GETTING LOST

Mishaps of an Accidental Nomad

GETTING LOST

Mishaps of an Accidental Nomad

by

DAVE FOX

INKWATER
PRESS

Portland • Oregon
INKWATERPRESS.COM

www.inkwaterpress.com

ISBN-13 978-1-59299-329-1
ISBN-10 1-59299-329-X

Publisher: Inkwater Press

2nd Edition

Printed in the U.S.A.
All paper is acid free and meets all ANSI standards for archival quality paper.
Printed on partially recycled and FSC and/or SFI certified paper.

TABLE OF CONTENTS

ACKNOWLEDGMENTS

I would like to thank my lovely wife for supporting me in writing this book. I really would like to thank my lovely wife, but… ummm…I'm still single, so never mind.

I would like to thank my agent for negotiating a six-figure book deal for me. Unfortunately, however, I don't have an agent either, nor a six-figure book deal.

Damn.

Personal note to my future agent: If I find out you've been sleeping with my future wife, you're fired.

There are some people who do exist whom I would like to thank. I am deeply grateful to Tim Bete, Teri Rizvi, and all the awesome volunteers at the Erma Bombeck Writers' Workshop, for helping this book come to life.

Thanks to Jeremy Solomon and Linda Weinerman at Inkwater Press for freeing me from the clutches of self-publishing and getting my words out into the big world. Also at Inkwater, thanks and a big, loud "Moo!" go to Masha Shubin for making this book look so sexy. Nobody's really sure why Masha decided to put a cow on the cover of a book that has absolutely nothing to do with cows, but I thank Masha for bestowing us all with such nostrilly bovine goodness.

Several friends have offered cultural and linguistic feedback:

Omar Ahmed, Lale Surmen Aran, Hanne Calonius, Theodoros Kazakos, Timur Leno, and Børre Lund. Other friends have been kind enough to slog through sections of my rough drafts or to share their thoughts on writing, publishing, and humor in general: Rebecca Agiewich, Erin Armstrong, Ben Benson, Amanda Castleman, Jeni Enns, Steve Fox, Susan Hodges, Dave Lieber, Maggie O'Neill, Michael Ross, Bill Stainton, Erin Stallings, Stu Stuart, and Dan and Nancy Wiggins.

Darbi Macy critiqued the manuscript so thoroughly, she deserves a big plate of chocolate chip cookies for her efforts. Sadly, she bakes much better cookies than I ever will, so that would be a lame way for me to thank her. Double thanks and a beer go to Rhonda Pelikan, who was unceremoniously forgotten in the first edition's acknowledgements. If I've forgotten anybody else, please accept my sincere apologies. Give my agent a call and he'll make sure you're in the next edition.

Special thanks to Marshall J. Cook, professor, mentor, and friend. I took Marshall's "Introduction to News Writing" class at the University of Wisconsin 19 years ago. He still hasn't managed to get rid of me.

Kathy Bradley, Barbara Sjoholm, and Seattle's Author Editor Clinic offered feedback on the rough draft and helped whittle the manuscript down to a digestible size.

My parents both helped spark memories for the early section of this book. They also offered to read the manuscript. Mom, Dad, thanks for offering. And please understand that no writer in his right mind would *ever* let his parents critique his work before it went to press. But I appreciate your enthusiasm and I thank you in advance for not disowning me when you read about the messes I've gotten myself into.

Tusen takk to my Norwegian family: Per and Tordis; Marius and Kari, Kaisa and Hillevi; Hanne, Wenche, and Johanna; and Thomas, for helping my time as a surrogate Norwegian reverberate far beyond the year I spent as an exchange student.

Rick Steves and the entire travel-obsessed crew at Rick Steves'

Europe have fueled my wanderlust for more than a decade. I can't imagine a better group of co-workers. Holly Johnson has helped me travel to more far-flung destinations on our planet. Cynthia Orr has offered brilliant business advice and tamed the voices in my head as needed.

Hugs and irritating snorky noises go to Kattina Rabdau for sticking around long enough to discover I really *am* weird enough.

Seattle's Wayward Coffeehouse has nourished me with caffeinated beverages and allowed me to sit in their establishment and write for hours on end. They have never kicked me out for acting crazy and shouting obscenities at my laptop. I thank them for that.

The Pig & Whistle Bar and Grill has nourished me with non-caffeinated beverages and sparkling conversation. Thanks especially to Celester Gray for making me feel like a rock star at my first book launch party. Naming a cocktail the "Getting Lost" was mighty flattering. (And yeah, a Scotch mojito is pretty freaking weird, but so is this book.)

Balderdash Books and Santoro's Books in Seattle, and the Edmonds Bookshop and the Savvy Traveler in Edmonds, Washington, were all kind enough to stock my first edition. Thanks for supporting a scroungy local author such as me, even when the high cost of self-publishing forced you to accept a lousy profit margin.

If I tried to list all of my friends, at home and abroad, who I should thank for their support and encouragement, this book would be way too long. So I can't mention you all by name, but you know who you are. Thanks guys.

Okay. Enough misty-eyed drivel. Let's get moving.

GETTING LOST

PART I

PREPARING FOR TAKE-OFF

1976-1977

In December, 1976, I almost started a riot in Northern Africa.

This, in and of itself, isn't so remarkable. The Middle East has a sad history of turbulence, and many people before me have caused much bigger messes than I almost did. But in 1976, I was only eight years old.

I wasn't a normal American kid.

Back home in America, many months earlier, my parents announced one night at dinner that they had a big surprise. But before they would tell me the big surprise, I had to clean my plate.

This was a problem.

I was a finicky eater as a child. Basically, if a meal didn't consist of Kellogg's Froot Loops, I wouldn't eat it. I made a special exception for pizza. This dietary restriction created challenges, mainly because my mother would not let me eat Froot Loops. "You'll get cancer," she'd say. So until sometime around puberty, I was on a hunger strike. Dinner each night became a staring contest: Me versus the Beef Stroganoff.

The standoff would often result in negotiations that could last as late as bedtime. "Just two more bites of carrots," my mom would propose. "Then you can have a cookie." Sometimes I'd give in, and put the evil vegetables in my mouth, scrunching up my face like a disgusted pug, then gulping my milk desperately to destroy the aftertaste. Sometimes, I'd just rearrange my food, making an

me on Fruit Loops

indentation where I would swear I had removed food from my plate and inserted it in my mouth. There were lots of things I liked to do as a child. Eating was not one of them.

On this particular night though, the night of the Big Surprise, my mother must have prepared something for dinner I was willing to eat. Ice cream, perhaps. I don't recall, but I do remember the mood was jovial.

"Should we tell them about the surprise?" my mom asked my dad.

"Sure," he replied. "We can tell them now."

In one final manipulative act, my parents negotiated for me to take two more big gulps of milk, or three small gulps (my choice). Then they revealed the news.

"How would you boys like to move to London for a year?" my dad asked.

"Yeah!" I shouted.

"Can I have a cookie?" my brother said.

Steve was three. He had no concept of London, but I did. I knew all about the place because two years earlier, my parents had gone there without me.

My grandmother came out to Maryland that week to make sure Steve and I didn't burn down the neighborhood. It was a fun time, with lots of stories, visits to the Smithsonian, and more treats than usual. When our parents returned home, they came bearing gifts, and tales of a faraway land with double-decker buses and policemen called "bobbies" who wore funny hats.

Now, two years later, they were offering to take me there. I was thrilled. I wanted to see Big Ben, and the changing of the guard at Buckingham Palace. I had no concept of how far away we'd be going.

I'm sure my parents breathed a sigh of relief when I expressed excitement about moving. They had tricked me, using one of the oldest parental con games: Ask a question with over-the-top zeal, and a child will answer yes. Yes, *of course* I wanted to move five time zones away from all of my friends, across an ocean, to a land where I would be singled out for talking funny, a land whose food was reputed to be even worse than America's.

The months that followed were full of anticipation and planning. We had some big issues to sort out before we could go. One night at dinner, after Steve had escaped from the table, my mother confided in me that she had a concern. It was about my brother, and getting through customs. The problem wasn't getting Steve through customs. It was getting Steve through customs with his blankie.

My brother was like Linus. He took his security blanket everywhere. And he didn't just carry it with him. He gnawed on it. He had his favorite corner, which was always in his mouth, with the occasional exception of at meal times. After three and a half years of getting chewed on, the blankie had taken on a certain odor. It was a sour smell, the scent of a three-year-old's breath. Mom would wash the blankie to keep it reasonably sanitary – usually against my brother's protests – but no matter how many extra-heavy-duty spin cycles she put it through, the chewed-on smell remained, like an indelible stain.

"I'm afraid they won't let us into the country if they smell it," my mom said. "But Steven will have a fit if we take it away. Maybe he won't notice if we get to London and it's gone."

My mother was wise to consult me on this issue. At age seven-and-a-half, I had more insight into the mind of a three-year-old than she did.

"He'll notice," I told her.

"Maybe we'll tell him he can't bring the whole thing," she suggested. "Maybe he could just bring a small piece of it. When he starts school, he's going to have to get by without it anyway."

I agreed this was a good solution.

We called Steve into the kitchen.

"David and I were just talking," my mom said. "You're getting to be so big! You're getting to be too big for your blankie."

Steve's face took on a horrified look. His lower lip started to tremble. My mom back-pedaled.

"Well, we were just thinking, your blankie's too big to take to England. But maybe we could cut off a corner of it."

Steve relaxed.

Then my mom did something really dumb. She let Steve choose which corner he could bring. Of course, he chose the smelly part.

The school year ended. Finally, August came, complete with a suitcase as big as me, and a lesson in how to sign my name in my passport. On our last night in Maryland, we stayed in a hotel. Our house was empty.

I couldn't sleep that night. I was too excited. I didn't know exactly what I was excited about. I was too young to comprehend the changes I was about to experience, but there was a buzz in the air. Something big was about to happen.

At five in the morning, my dad looked over at me. I thought I was in trouble for being awake, but we both got out of bed and sat in the far corner of the hotel room, away from my mother and snoring brother. We whispered about what the day would be like.

Twenty-four hours later, we touched down at Heathrow. Steve and his blankie made it through customs. So did the rest of us.

As I stepped into the first few moments of my new life as a foreigner, I felt stunned. For months, my parents had been teaching me everything they knew about England, but they had neglected one huge piece of information. Everybody – every single person in the entire city of London – was a butler or a nanny. I was dumbfounded, but that was the only explanation. I had watched lots of cartoons in my day, and the only people who spoke with accents like that were servants named Chauncey. Everybody talked so funny in London. It didn't cross my mind that I was the one who was different.

I've been different ever since. My parents' plan had been to bounce overseas for a year, have a fun cultural experience, and then return home to Bethesda, Maryland, where normal American life would resume. But it doesn't work that way. You can't take a geeky American kid to live in a foreign country for a year, shuttle him around to a bunch of other foreign countries during that year, and then expect him to be normal when he returns home. His American roots have been partially clipped, supplanted with new sprouts that grow toward faraway places.

One year after arriving in London, we would cross the ocean back to the US. I would touch down in Washington, DC, talking like Chauncey the butler. I would shed my new accent quickly, so as to avoid torment from my American peers, but funny cartoon butler voice or not, never again would I feel completely American. I was like a salivating poodle who had just tasted fresh sirloin for the first time. I would spend the rest of my life yipping for more, wagging my tail at any hint of new opportunities for culture shock.

Whether in America or overseas, I've been a partial foreigner most of my life. Over time, I've developed a philosophy about foreign travel: "When you travel, things go wrong."

As a professional tour guide, I share this philosophy with my groups on our first night together. They smile, waiting for the uplifting second part, the part where I reassure them that with me as their guide, everything will be just fine. But I can't make that promise. No honest tour guide can. Venturing into foreign turf is begging for things to go awry. When we wander far from home, it's easy to forget we are the ones who are different, not the people whose neighborhoods we are visiting. We don't know the local rules. Occasionally, we make a mess of things. So why travel if there is such potential for chaos? Because it beats staying home and watching Jerry Springer.

I've spent my life chasing confusion in foreign places. I've returned from trips with bruises, scars, diarrhea, and nervous breakdowns. I've been stranded, robbed, threatened with machine guns, charged by irate sheep, burned by volcanoes, scowled at by angry mobs, and fed airline food. None of these experiences were pleasant in the moment, but over time, travel mishaps evolve into our funniest stories.

Anthropologists and travel writers have debated for years the ethics of dropping into a foreign place and writing about people from an outsider's perspective. Is it fair for me to show up in a culture where I don't know what I'm doing, get myself embroiled in a situation where things go all wonky, and then zip back home to write a tongue-in-cheek account of what happened? When we write about foreign cultures, particularly with a humorous approach, we risk misunderstanding. We risk offending. That's not what I want to do. I travel in part because I believe meeting people from other places makes our planet a happier planet.

So before we go any further, let's make one thing clear: Every place I write about in this book is a place I love – even the places where events seemed catastrophic at the time. I write all of these tales with the utmost respect for the people who live in the countries where I have been a guest and a stranger.

This book is a collection of my favorite international travel mishaps and cultural conundrums. Some of the stories are interconnected. Others are random moments in random places. People sometimes ask me if they are 100 percent true, and I tell them they are as true as my memory allows. In a few instances, names have been changed to protect the guilty. In a few other instances, names have been changed because I forgot the names.

My North African riot? I'm getting to that, but we'll begin a few months earlier, in England. So climb aboard and follow me. No seatbelts required.

THE WAY-BACK MACHINE

LEWISHAM, ENGLAND

W e were driving down the sidewalk in Lewisham, England. It was our first family outing in the fluorescent orange station wagon that came with the house we were renting. Steve and I were in what we called "the way-back" – the very back part of the car, where there were no seats, just a flat, fuzzy slab intended for cargo or sheepdogs. It was our favorite place to sit.

Our mom was up front in the passenger seat, having the most stressful ride of her life. She was stressed because some fool had put the steering wheel on *her* side of the car. She was having her first ever lesson in driving on the left.

Her highly qualified instructor was our dad. He had nearly two full hours of left-hand driving experience. He was sitting in the driver's seat, which had no steering wheel or pedals, but that wasn't stopping him from trying to control the vehicle. His driving method consisted of wrapping his fingers around the door handle with a 12-ton grip, and issuing helpful instructions to our mother, such as, "Be careful!" and "Oh shit!" His use of the S-word was something new. Steve and I had not been aware our father knew this word. It made us giggle.

In an effort to quell our giggling, Dad yelled at us to be quiet because we were making our mother nervous. This caused us to laugh harder, which caused our mother to get more nervous, which caused our dad to freak out some more.

"Well," Dad said as we pulled up in front of the house, "that wasn't bad for a first effort." And although I'm not sure I'd agree, both of my parents did quickly master the art of driving on the other side of the road with two cackling monsters in the way-back. During our entire year in England, neither of my parents caused a single traffic fatality. The guy on the motorcycle recovered, and I swear his injuries weren't my mom's fault.

The motorcycle accident happened many months into our year. It was one of our more interesting evenings. I can still replay the film in my mind.

In countries where you drive on the left, you are supposed to pass on the right. If you are a tough biker dude in a leather jacket, however, you are exempt from all traffic laws.

So we were driving to the grocery store – Mom behind the steering wheel, Steve and me in the way back, Dad safely at work in Greenwich – when a guy on a motorcycle attempted to pass us on the left side of the car. This might have worked, had there not been a sidewalk next to us, but…well…here's a motorcycle safety tip for you: If there's a foot of space between the sidewalk and a moving vehicle, do not attempt to squeeze between that vehicle and the sidewalk unless you want to impress your cool motorcycle dude friends with a new set of scars.

It was one of those moments you recall in slow motion for years to come. I saw the biker come up from behind and coast in my mom's blind spot. I saw him attempt a couple of times to squeeze between us and the sidewalk. I saw him make his move. I heard the thud against our car door. I watched him fly off of his bike onto the pavement.

I still remember how I reacted. "Mom," I half-shouted, half-whispered from the back of the car, "drive away before anyone notices!"

And to this day, I still think that would have been the prudent decision. Within a few months of arriving in England, Steve and I had started to pick up British accents, but our parents were still talking like a couple of foreigners. And here's the thing about being American and getting in an accident in England: Everybody assumes it's your fault.

"Those Yanks, they drive on the wrong side of the road in America, don't they?"

"Why yes, I believe they do. They're a strange lot, the Americans."

So our mom, who couldn't have noticed the guy on the motorbike trying to pass illegally, explained to me as calmly as could be expected, that she couldn't just drive off, and that Steve and I were to sit silently in the car while she waited for the police to come take her away forever, leaving my brother and me to starve to death in the way-back.

Instead of doing the right thing in terms of self-preservation, she did the right thing in terms of obeying the law. She got out of the car.

I still remember clearly the biker's first words. "You bloody shithead!" he screeched at my mother. Two thoughts passed through my mind: How could a tough biker dude shriek in such a shrill, high-pitched voice? He sounded like a girl. Also, why was he calling my mother a bloody shithead when *he* was the one who was bleeding?

Mom was apologizing, and trembling. A crowd of shoppers and shopkeepers began to gather. The beauty of it was they were comforting my mother rather than the motorcyclist lying mangled on the pavement. Mom was visibly shaken – far more than the fallen biker, who seemed more concerned with teaching us all some new British vocabulary than he was with his injuries. I remember a butcher with a big knife in his hand telling our mother he had seen the whole thing and it wasn't her fault. I remember the words "American driver" getting tossed around by the growing crowd. Most of all, I remember the ambulance.

The ambulance arrived with its two-tone British siren blaring, and its front windshield broken into several thousand tiny pieces. All several thousand of those tiny pieces were still sitting precariously in the window's frame in a shatter-resistant state. The driver, unable to see through the broken glass, was craning his neck out the side window to see where he was going.

On the way to the accident, the ambulance had gotten into a collision of its own. I'm not sure what the details were. I guessed the ambulance driver must have done what I had told my mother to do: drive away before anyone notices. You'd think he would have called for a different ambulance, but no. Instead, this wounded ambulance, its windshield broken into thousands of tiny pieces, came roaring up to the scene of our accident, and parked, nose-to-nose, directly in front of our car.

"She hit the motorbike *and the ambulance?*" I heard somebody ask. "How did she manage to hit the bloody ambulance?"

"Well, listen to her. She sounds American."

"Oh, she's an *American*, is she? I hear they drive on the wrong side of the road in America."

In 1976, *Starsky and Hutch* was one of the big hit TV shows in England. It didn't do a lot for the perception of American drivers. But in the end, everything worked out okay. The police assured my mom that the biker had been passing illegally, and that she had nothing to worry about. The rest of the incident was resolved by telephone.

The motorcyclist was pretty lucky. He walked away with only a broken wrist and some contusions, and probably a good story he still tells today about the bloody American lunatic who was driving so legally, she almost killed him.

One of the paramedics borrowed a policeman's billy club, and used it to knock the shattered glass out of the windshield so they could see where they were going and drive back to the hospital with the wind in their hair.

Mom eventually stopped shaking and made it through the rest of the year with a perfect driving record.

And I scored big time. We never made it to the grocery store that evening. We went out for dinner to my favorite restaurant and ate pizza.

HOW CAN YOU HAVE ANY PUDDING IF YOU DON'T EAT YOUR MEAT?

LEWISHAM, ENGLAND

They didn't serve pizza for lunch at school in England. My hunger strike continued.

We'd been living in our new house for a couple of weeks when the first day of school arrived. I was a "first year junior." Translation: third grade. I was relieved we had not come to England any sooner. Had I been in second grade, I would have been placed in "infant school," a term that sounded horribly degrading for an almost-seven-year-old. But I was almost eight, in with the big kids, the juniors.

Lunch never crossed my mind as my mother accompanied me on the one-block stroll to school the first day. Lunch to me was unnecessary.

In America, I had always brought my lunch to school, except on Fridays, when the school menu was cheese pizza for 55 cents. Most other days, I subsisted on peanut butter and jelly on Wonder Bread, in an un-politically-correct Hong Kong Phooey lunchbox, along with a banana, and a couple of cookies that always tasted like the banana after several hours of lunchbox marinating. Along with my packed lunch every morning, I received eight cents to spend on a carton of chocolate milk, which I eventually learned I could use to bolster my quarter-a-week allowance if I did so discreetly.

How Can You Have Any Pudding if
You Don't Eat Your Meat?

But in England, things worked differently. There was no milk money. At 10:30 each morning, there was a milk break, which consisted of an eager race to the cafeteria for free, government-subsidized milk in little glass bottles with red foil lids. We'd shake the bottles to mix the creamy part at the top with the less creamy part at the bottom. Then the cafeteria lady would hand us a thin straw to pierce through the foil lid. We'd walk back to class slurping. When someone stayed home sick, there were extra bottles of milk, which would be handed out as seconds to a few lucky students. Why the other kids fought over something as repulsive as milk was baffling to me, but I joined in the ritual so as not to be an outsider.

It was milk at 10:30 and dinner at noon. That made no sense. Dinner was what you ate at 6 p.m., but the British children were strange. They had dinner at lunch time. Then they'd "eat their tea" after school at four. This confused the lingo in my pseudo-American household, where I was working hard to use the proper local vocabulary. We stuck to an American eating schedule, which meant I got dinner at noon at school, and dinner at six at home. I couldn't visit friends at four because they were eating their tea, and they couldn't visit me at six because I was eating my second dinner. I read a lot of books that year.

School dinner and home dinner had two things in common: They were both the biggest meal of the day, and they both lacked pizza. At home it was the same ritual as before, back in America. Food was put before me. I resisted. Negotiations ensued. At school, it was much more violent.

The Brits have contributed many great things to society: pub culture, Shakespeare, the Beatles, soccer hooligans. They are also known for their cuisine, but not in a good way. I still remember what they served for dinner on my first day of school. It was "shepherd's pie with smashed potatoes and greens." For dessert, there was rice pudding, which struck me as downright cruel. Rice was a vehicle for soy sauce. It didn't belong in pudding. Furthermore,

15

meat didn't belong in pie, and pie for the main course made less sense than dinner at noon.

School dinner consisted of lining up, class by class, with a plate and a tray, and moving through the line as the cafeteria ladies slopped food on your plate. It was like you see in movies about prison, only this was worse because at school, they didn't just give you the food; they made you swallow it.

I tried to find a way out. In America, when I didn't feel like eating my banana (which was always), I'd just wait until the teachers weren't looking and fling it into the trash. But the British school system wasn't so liberal. Once you navigated the food line, you had to choose a table. You could sit anywhere you liked. Teachers ate with the students. I learned quickly that where I sat could have a profound impact – positive or negative – on the outcome of my starvation quest.

Whenever possible, I'd sit near Mark. I didn't particularly like Mark, but Mark liked food. He was a human garbage disposal, and he'd scarf down whatever you offered him. You didn't want to get caught trading plates with Mark, or the teachers would make you finish *everything* on your plate while they lectured you about the poor starving children in India. But if you were stealthy, you could make the switch.

The person to avoid sitting with was Mr. Bennett, but sometimes, the seat next to him was the only one left. Mr. Bennett taught a class of fourth year juniors. He was the only human being who ate faster than Mark. He expected the students to keep up with him. Mr. Bennett had a particular love for salt. The salt shakers were made of glass, with white plastic tops that funneled into a single exit point. The hole was a full millimeter across, which meant you couldn't shake the shaker over your food or the salt would pour out too fast. Instead, the protocol was to pour a little salt into your palm, then take a pinch and sprinkle it on your food. But Mr. Bennett did things differently. He would turn the shaker upside down, letting the salt flow freely as he did two or three laps around his meat and vegetables. Then he would attack.

HOW CAN YOU HAVE ANY PUDDING IF YOU DON'T EAT YOUR MEAT?

Mr. Bennett ate with the uniquely British skill of balancing food atop his upside-down fork and shoveling it into his mouth, or using his potatoes as edible cement to help his peas stick to the knife so he could lick them off. He was fast and determined. It didn't take long before all of his food had swirled together into a puke-colored school dinner stew. Flavor meant nothing to Mr. Bennett. Food was food, and it needed to go into his stomach before any of those poor starving children from India showed up and tried to wrestle it away it from him.

When you were finished eating, or thought you were, there was no place to dispose of the remainder of your meal. Instead, you had to raise your hand, sometimes keeping it up until your shoulder ached before anyone noticed you. Eventually, a teacher or one of the cafeteria ladies would come inspect the remains of your dinner and decide whether to grant you dessert authorization, or whether to torture you longer.

I learned quickly that raising my hand haphazardly was like Russian roulette. The trick was to scrutinize the teachers' locations, and wait for one of the kind ones to look your way – someone who would let you go without a lot of negotiating. The petite female teachers were best. They didn't mind if you left half your meal.

The cafeteria ladies were smarter than the petite teachers. It was best to avoid them when negotiating your exit. School dinner was their life, and they had been in the biz too long to be fooled by the old "hide your fish sticks under the smashed potatoes" ploy. This was a maximum security cafeteria, and if they suspected any attempts to conceal food or transfer it to Mark, they would sit down next to you and watch you eat. By the end of the school year, I had gotten to know the cafeteria ladies pretty well.

Their intentions were good. They just wanted to see their children well-nourished. When it wasn't dinner time, and I'd pass them in the halls, I liked the cafeteria ladies and they liked me, but when it came to eating, our friendship was irrelevant.

"I'm full," I would say.

"But David, you've hardly touched your lima beans."

"Yes I have," I would try, going with a literal interpretation.

"No David, you must eat more. Look at you. Don't you want to grow?"

I hated that question. Of course I wanted to grow. All my life, I'd been the short kid. My peers, particularly back in America, found cruel ways to remind me of this. "Your manipulative questions are detrimental to my self-esteem," I wanted to tell the cafeteria ladies, but at age eight, I couldn't find the words.

So I'd say no. No, I didn't want to grow. And if lima beans were the solution, I really meant it.

I'd sit and watch my food. The ladies would sit and watch me watching my food. Sometimes it would get unbearable. I really would try to put more food in my mouth, just to end the scrutiny, but I was a small kid being force fed two dinners a day. Good food or bad, it was tough getting it down. Occasionally, they'd notice this.

"Oh David," they'd finally say with a touch of sympathy, "you're struggling."

I didn't know what they meant by this. I wanted to know. I wanted to know how to struggle, because when I struggled, they'd take pity on me and declare a truce and set me free. But I didn't know how to struggle. It was something I did involuntarily. Occasionally, I'd get lucky and start struggling. But usually, we got into the same negotiations I had at home.

"Just a few more bites, David. Then you can have your pudding."

"Pudding" was British for dessert in the same way people in some southern US states refer to all soft drinks as "Coke." Collectively, rice pudding was called "pudding," sponge cake was called "pudding," treacle was called "pudding," even apples were called "pudding." I found that last item particularly offensive. Fruit had no business being a dessert choice.

If this is sounding familiar, it's from "Another Brick in the Wall" by Pink Floyd. "If you don't eat your meat,

apple pudding

you can't have any pudding! How can you have any pudding if you don't eat your meat?" I'm pretty certain the band hired Mr. Bennett to read those lines.

After lunch, I'd go out to play, unless the dinner standoff had endured through recess. In the beginning, I was a celebrity on the playground.

In the eyes of an English eight-year-old, America was one big Disney World, with the added bonus of high-speed car chases and the Fonz. *Starsky and Hutch* and *Happy Days* were the two big shows on British television. Starsky came on after my bedtime, which caused problems because it meant my British peers knew more about American culture than I did.

"Everyone in America has guns," they'd explain to me. "And big cars. How big is your car?"

I had no clue. I'd never measured.

I tried to be polite, but the attention grew tiresome. In my first few weeks of school, everyone wanted to play with the American. A small crowd would follow me around the playground. They'd fight over me.

"He's going to play football with us," the alpha-male of one clique would say.

"He is not! He promised to play 'had' with us."

"Had" was the British word for "tag."

"You said you were going to play had with us, right David?"

"Ummm, yeah."

"But you told me you wanted to play football," the leader of the rival faction would retort. "You *promised*."

And I did. I promised everyone I would play with them. I was too polite to say no. I'd triple book my social life, wishing the other kids would notice the pressure I was under and give me a break.

"I think I'm going to go sit on the bench for a while," I would say, hoping at least some of them would get bored and leave.

"He wants to have a sit-down," Jonathan would explain to everyone else. "And he wants *me* to sit next to him."

After a few weeks, my status faded. I was starting to become a normal British school kid. By December, I was even beginning to lose my American accent – just a little.

But not enough.

It was time for the school Christmas pantomime. The teachers had a special part for me.

MASCULINITY SAVED!

LEWISHAM, ENGLAND

N oddy and Big Ears never made it in America. Noddy was a toy with a nodding head. Big Ears was an elf. They went on adventures that sparked children's imagination and taught the value of friendship. They were the creations of one of Britain's most treasured and prolific children's authors, Enid Blyton, and they were heroes to the children of England. But Blyton's stories about them never flew in America. The books were banned because, according to the BBC, Noddy and Big Ears had a relationship that some Americans considered "implicitly homosexual."

So spending my first seven years in America, I had not been exposed to the allegedly perverted elf-and-toy duo who had won the hearts of British school children. When November rolled around, and it was time to rehearse for the school Christmas pantomime, I didn't know what I was in for.

"Noddy and Big Ears' Adventures in Toyland" was a full-on musical production with virtually every student in four grades playing a role or singing in the choir. I came running home one day to tell my mom.

"I'm going to be a nole!" I said.

"What's a nole?" she asked.

I had no clue.

She looked it up in the dictionary. There was no definition.

"I think it might start with a 'K'" I told her.

She looked up knole and found "knoll – a small rounded mound or hill."

"You're going to be a hill?"

I was perplexed. I had heard of kids being cast as trees in school plays, but a clump of dirt seemed rather dull.

We had another meeting at school a few days later. I came home with fresh information.

"I'm not going to be a knoll. I'm going to be a gnome!"

"Oh!" my mother said. "How exciting!"

"What's a gnome?" I asked. I felt happy when she told me. An elf was more interesting than a hill. The news eased the sting of some other, humiliating information I had to convey.

"They told us we have to wear tights."

I was eight. I was oblivious to what Noddy and Big Ears might be doing in bed late at night, but I had learned enough in America about gender roles to know that boys did not wear tights.

"Lots of us have to," I explained, hoping my mother wouldn't think I was a sissy. What I really didn't get was none of the other kids seemed to mind. Even the tough boys, the ones who started fights and talked about cars, had taken the announcement in stride.

My mother's first response was to reassure me there was nothing to be embarrassed about. Lots of men wore tights. Ballet dancers, for example.

I cringed. "There are men who are ballet dancers?"

"David, things are just a little bit different here. I think it's okay for boys to wear tights in England. Children play in them. Anyway, none of your friends in Maryland are going to know."

So while I was at school one day, my mom went out and bought me a pair. They were a good masculine shade of brown. She went for the more expensive packaging because it pictured children – girls *and boys* – playing together in tights.

"See?" my mom said, pointing to the picture. "It's okay for boys to wear them here."

I tried them on. I felt like the same person I had always been. I began getting comfortable with the idea that they were just a different kind of clothing, but my brother quickly disposed of that notion. He made up a new song. He sang it to me. It was called "David Wears Tights All the Time."

I chased Steve up the stairs, but he slammed his bedroom door before I could injure him. So then I did what any red-blooded eight-year-old boy would do if his masculinity was being challenged by his little brother. I burst into tears.

"David wears tights all the time," Steve crooned through his bedroom door. "David wears tights all the *tiiiiime!*"

It wasn't a particularly imaginative song. Those were the only lyrics. But considering Steve was four, you had to admire his ingenuity. The song served its purpose.

As rehearsals progressed, I didn't discuss the humiliation with my friends. I wanted to ask them, "Are you really going to wear tights?" But the other boys seemed unconcerned. I tried to act cool. We'd stay late after school each day – those of us with even minor acting parts – going over our lines in our street clothes. As mid-December approached, Mr. Bennett pulled me aside one day. He had a special role for me.

I'd been living in England for three months now. In England, I never got teased for being the shortest kid in class like I did in America because, face it, my American accent was a far more interesting target. All you could do to a short kid was beat him up. But if you cornered a kid with a foreign accent, you could mimic him. If you did it well*, you would win the admiration of your mates while the American kid cringed and told you, ordered you, pleaded with you to shut up.

There were days when I left school in tears because of this. Mr. Bennett must have seen what was

*which, at age eight, you did not, but to British third-graders trying to sound American, anything vaguely resembling a prepubescent John Wayne twang would do

23

going on. He was about to make me a hero. I was being type-cast for my American accent.

There were bad guys afoot in Toyland. Some of the older kids rode motorcycles. Other kids *were* the motorcycles. And I seem to recall some evil bats. The older kids played the bad guys. I envied them, if for no other reason than that the bikers got to wear jeans and white T-shirts, like the Fonz.

The bikers, or the bats, or some other gnome-hating terrorist organization, were out to destroy Noddy and Big Ears and ruin Christmas. I was to swoop in with the line that would save everybody: "In these woods, there'll be no danger. I'm the famous Gnome Ranger!"

Mr. Bennett coached me on the lines – on the timing, on the inflection. "You have to project," he told me. His advice was more welcomed than "If you don't eat your meat, you can't have any pudding." I was starting to like him.

As opening (and closing) night approached, the news got even better. I would get to wear a cowboy hat. And a badge. And a holster with a gun. For a whole musical sequence immediately following my line, I would walk around and shoot the audience. I felt manly now, in spite of the tights.

On the night of the big show, my pun brought the house down. My accent had already begun morphing into British English, but it was still American enough to work. The school gymnasium exploded with laughter. I got more applause than Noddy and Big Ears. I shot my neighbor. I shot my parents. I shot Steve multiple times.

I learned some important lessons from my acting debut:

1) Sometimes being a foreigner is a good thing. It can land you a starring role.

2) People who worry about the sexual mores of elves and nodding-head toys have way too much time on their hands.

3) If you must wear tights, always carry a gun.

SOUL SURVIVORS

HAMMAMET, TUNISIA

I didn't want to go on a camel ride. I had heard too many horror stories.

Camels were mean. They spat. They bit. They ran terrorist training camps.

At age eight, my mind had not yet been corrupted by paranoid stereotypes about Arab people. But *camels* were a different story. My parents, not realizing they were traumatizing me, had told me the tale of an American woman in Egypt whose camel had been bitten by another camel. This caused the American woman's camel to freak out and gallop into the desert with its terrified tourist screaming from atop the hump.

help!

"You'll be fine," my parents coaxed. "Look, their mouths are tied closed so they can't bite or spit."

That was true. The camels had muzzles crafted out of twine, but I didn't care. I was refusing to get on. In the end, it was my brother who shamed me into climbing aboard. Steve loved animals. Riding a camel was his Tunisian highlight. I couldn't let my little brother humiliate me with his bravery. I was still reeling from the gnome-in-tights incident.

Camels are tall animals – much taller than horses. Mounting

them is no easy feat. You must first convince the camel to kneel so you can climb aboard. "Nice camel," you must say to the camel. "Be a good beast and get down on your knees."

Sometimes the camel will not want to get down on its knees. The animal might need a bit of coaxing. "You can do it," you might say. "Do not make me raise my voice, camel."

But sometimes you must raise your voice. "Camel! Get down on your knees NOW or it will be camel fricassee for dinner tonight!"

Eventually the camel will kneel and let you climb aboard. Then the camel will laugh at you because he knows what's coming next. The camel must now stand up before he can take you anywhere, but camels don't stand up gracefully. They straighten their hind legs first, still kneeling in the front. This causes you to lurch forward and sob with terror.

At least that's the effect it was having on me. As I clung to the saddle, my hump-backed monster rose on his back legs and then hesitated. He was refusing to stand upright in front. My arms shuddered as I struggled to hold on. I was leaning forward at a precarious angle, about to tumble head first, down the camel's neck, over his head, onto the sand, where he was going to find a way out of his muzzle and eat me.

"I'm going to fall off!" I was screaming.

"You're not going to fall off," my mother said. "Just hang on."

I didn't fall off, though once my camel finally stood up straight, I wished I had. With Mom and me on one animal, Dad and Steve on another, and our dromedary chauffeur on a third, we began lumbering along the beach.

Camels walk with an awkward swagger. They're slow versions of those four-legged robots that gallop through the desert in *Star Wars*. They move with a bounce, like lethargic, mechanical bulls, the main difference being that if you fall off a mechanical bull, it will not spit at you afterward and stomp victoriously on your head.

I was whimpering. Steve was giggling – in part because he was having fun on the camel, in part because he was having fun watching me whimper. I just wanted to go back to the hotel and play pinball.

We were in Hammamet, which in 1976 was a dusty Mediterranean village struggling to become a resort town. Two beach-front hotels catered to English holidaymakers whose primary goal in Tunisia was to avoid all things Tunisian. Without leaving the hotel compound, they could swim in the pools, steam in the hammam, play backgammon, dominoes, and miniature golf, and refresh themselves in one of several hotel bars. There were pinball machines and pool tables in a room managed by a friendly man who stood about four feet tall if you counted his fez. A restaurant served three meals a day. It didn't matter what you ordered. Everything, including the delicious-looking chocolate cakes, tasted like rancid olive oil.

We were different from the other tourists though. We weren't spending our week cowering by the pool. We took day trips to bustling Tunis, historic Carthage, and fashionable Sidi Bou Saïd. On this particular day, we were on a mission to discover the real Hammamet.

The medina was a small walled city that, until the 1920s, had enclosed Hammamet completely. It was a mile and a half from the tourist zone. In recent decades, Hammamet had ballooned beyond its city walls. Near the medina, small stucco houses sprang up along dirt roads. Itching to capitalize on their palm tree beaches, the residents had begun developing a resort area too, but they built their hotels away from their original town center, sequestering tourists a healthy distance from their village.

Our camels turned off the beach, through a gate, onto a dirt road that led toward the real town. We were riding into a world I'd never seen before. I marveled at the stop signs that looked just like American ones, only with Arabic script. I began to relax, and pay attention to things other than the fact that I was about to die.

We rode through a residential area. Housewives in headscarves swept their front porches with homemade brooms crafted from sticks. Children smiled and waved to us. Everybody looked happy and poor, which confused me.

I couldn't grasp how poverty and palm trees could co-exist.

Bethesda, Maryland, didn't have palm trees, nor did Lewisham, England. The only place I had ever seen a palm tree was on television. They grew in places of opulence – places you went if you were a millionaire or a TV game show winner. When we had arrived at midnight a few nights prior, the first thought in my head had been, "Tunisians must be very rich." Only rich people had palm trees.

It took a while for the contrast to set in: tropical plants and sandy beaches that stayed warm even in December; large families in small houses who made their own brooms because they couldn't afford to buy brooms in a store. The two didn't go together. My mind was opening up to a new reality.

The camel driver took us to his home. It was a two-room house. He and his wife slept in the bedroom. His two children, somewhere between my age and Steve's, slept together in the living room on a twin bed that doubled as a sofa when visitors came. I smiled nervously at his children, and they did the same back to me. We couldn't converse. They spoke only Arabic, and translating from Arabic to French to English was too arduous for the adults. The adults drank tea. Steve and I got juice and cookies.

The juice was fresh-squeezed – straight from the citrus grove outside. This man didn't just sell camel rides to tourists. He was also a farmer. Behind his house were a ramshackle barn and more than a hundred citrus trees – oranges, lemons, tangerines. The man lifted me up to pick a tangerine. Then he took pity on me and hoisted me back onto the standing camel so I wouldn't have to repeat my earlier near-death experience. He ferried us back to the touristy section of town.

"I want to go again!" Steve announced as soon as we were off our camels.

I poked a stick through a beached jellyfish and flung it at him.

Steve woke me early the next morning.

"Merry Christmas," he said.

I told him to go back to sleep.

"But Santa was here. It's Christmas."

"It is not," I scolded, half asleep.

Steve jumped out of bed. He shoved a toy camel in front of me.

"Look what he brought us!"

I was shocked. My four-year-old brother was stealing camels?

"Steven! Where did you get that?"

"It's for you. It's from Santa. I got one too, see?"

Then I remembered. It *was* Christmas. Sort of. We had celebrated early – on December 19 in England before leaving for the airport. As far as I was concerned, Christmas was done for the year, but today was December 25.

The Hotel Fourati had no chimney for Santa to slide down, and for reasons I couldn't grasp, Tunisians didn't celebrate Christmas anyway, so I hadn't expected anything. In the afternoon, though, the other big hotel in the village hosted a party for the British and French kids on vacation with their parents.

There were games and snacks. Santa Claus came. In proper Arab style, he showed up late. Or, I shouldn't say late. Arabs have an expression: *"Insha'Allah"* – "God willing." What time does the bus leave? At 2:30, *Insha'Allah*, which means sometime between 1:30 and next April. Westerners freak out at this laid-back scheduling. It's not what we're used to. But if you live in a culture that operates on that sort of time frame, you shrug your shoulders and drink some more tea.

A crowd of us was gathered outside the hotel – French kids, English kids, and two lost Americans. We craned our necks, looking for him down the street. After much anticipation, Father Christmas appeared. He arrived on a camel. He wore a red outfit with white thermal underwear exposed from his knees down, and a beard of yellow cotton balls that covered his mouth and nose. It looked more like a cotton ball veil than a beard. He spoke three words of English: "Ho, ho, ho."

"I don't think that's really Santa," Steve whispered.

Well, yes, he was correct. The overgrown yellow beard, the reindeer with a hump and no antlers, the lack of English skills, were a giveaway, even to a four-year-old. I appreciated the effort nonetheless. Christmas wasn't a Tunisian holiday, but the hotel staff understood its cultural importance to Western children. We were on their turf, but for a few hours, they shared in our culture.

That night, there was a lavish Christmas feast in the hotel dining room. My dad ordered two servings of raw oysters – one for me, and one for him.

"I don't want oysters!" I whined. "I hate oysters." I had never seen an oyster before, let alone eat one, but I hated them anyway.

"They're not for you," my dad said. "They're for me."

"You said one for you and one for me," I protested. How stupid did he think I was?

"That's right," he said. "First I'm going to eat mine. Then I'm going to eat yours. I really like oysters."

I didn't believe him. I looked at my mom.

She was eyeing my dad like he was insane. She was cautious about what she ate. Raw anything seemed risky. Sanitary standards in Tunisia were not at the level our bodies were accustomed to.

"Pete, you're going to get sick," my mom said.

"I'll be fine," my dad said.

The waiter arrived with the oysters. I complained some more. I was still convinced this was an evil plot. My dad moved my plate next to him to shut me up. He started gobbling down order number one. "These are delicious," he said.

"I'm not eating any," I whined.

"Good," my dad said. "I'm going to eat them."

The next morning, my father woke up feverish and vomiting. Steve, who had eaten two of my dad's oysters in yet another attempt to outdo me, had a touch of food poisoning too. I was secretly pleased.

We moved Steve into my parents' room to play and puke. Then my mom and I set off down the beach. We had no goal in mind.

We just started walking. An hour later, we found ourselves at the medina.

A beggar sat at the entrance. I remembered him from a few days earlier. He had approached us in a café. He said nothing. He just pointed down at his feet, which pointed inward toward each other rather than straight ahead. Then he held out his hand. I had never seen a beggar before, nor had I encountered such a physical deformity.

We wandered through the market. There were toy drums for sale. I wanted to buy one with my allowance, but I had learned by now not to point, not to show any interest in anything. The shop-keepers were aggressive. If they caught you eyeing something, they would reel you into their shop. The next thing you knew, you'd be haggling over something you didn't want in the first place. I had gotten my parents in trouble several times already. If a shopkeeper saw me or Steve looking at something, he'd be all over our parents, doing everything he could to lure us into his shop. These guys were good. They could hard-sell my parents and smile encouragingly to me at the same time. It had taken me a few days to understand their game, but now I got it.

So we walked, looking as nonchalant as an American mother and her pale-skinned eight-year-old son can look wandering through an ancient North African market. We came upon a square, where a crowd was gathering. We stopped to see what was happening.

The square erupted in music. Dancers in ceremonial outfits emerged from a second floor doorway, singing, twirling, drum-ming their way down an exterior staircase. As their music filled the square, the crowd swelled. I wanted to get a better look.

I wandered away from my mother – not far, maybe 10 feet. She could still see me. I was safe.

I lifted my camera and peered through the viewfinder. I didn't bother framing the shot. I hadn't learned to do that yet. I just clicked.

Suddenly, the drumming, the singing, the danc-ing all stopped. The sound morphed in a matter of seconds from a happy celebration to a dull groan to a suspicious murmur that buzzed through the square.

I had no idea what I had just done. I noticed the change in mood on the square. I halfway noticed dozens of eyes burning angrily into my head, but I paid no attention. I wondered what was going on. Some fool had just caused a commotion of some kind, and boy, was he in trouble!

While all of this was happening, a little Tunisian girl about my age was having a chat with my mother in French.

"Is that your son over there?" the girl asked.

"*Oui,*" my mother replied.

"You'd better get out of here," the girl said.

I wandered back to my mother, still smiling. She grabbed me and flung me into a nearby taxi. "Hotel Fourati," she said to the driver.

"But Mom, why are we leaving?" I whined. I hadn't bought my drum yet.

"It's dinner time," my mother lied. "And we should see how Dad and Steve are doing."

I protested the whole way back to the hotel.

The color was back in my father's face when we arrived. "Did you have a good day?" he asked.

"We went back to the medina," I said. Then I complained about my drum. "You promised me I could get one."

My parents were smart enough not to discuss this with me before they had conferred privately. I was right; a promise had been made. My dad knew my mom wasn't going to deny me the drum I had been saving my pocket money for unless there was some good reason, such as that I almost got us both mangled by an angry mob. I was sent to the bathroom to wash my hands for dinner. When I emerged, my father was telling my mother not to worry.

"Don't worry about what?" I asked.

"Oh, nothing," they lied.

I can't remember how I dragged it out of them, but somehow I got my parents to explain what was going on. Calmly, they told me I shouldn't have taken that picture.

"Why not?"

They weren't sure. In some cultures farther south on the African continent, there were people who believed that if you took their picture, you were stealing their soul. My parents speculated that perhaps there was a similar belief here.*

*Tunisians actually have no such superstition, nor is there a problem with picture taking in mainstream Islam, but when you are a parent traveling with an eight-year old, your responsibility, in the eyes of the eight-year-old, is to have an immediate answer for everything. Stolen souls were the most plausible story my parents could come up with on the spot.

Mom and Dad reassured me everything was fine. I hadn't meant any harm; furthermore the souls of the people I had photographed couldn't really fit in my small, plastic camera.

I interpreted things differently. The change in energy on the square earlier began to register with me now. Had I been the cause of that? My fear started percolating, until it boiled into sheer panic. I was an unwitting fugitive on the lam, being hunted by half the population of Hammamet. They were all looking for the American kid. The healthy, non-food-poisoned one with the camera. Despite my parents' reassurances, I was convinced they were coming to get me.

I wasn't fearful of my personal safety so much as the safety of my camera. It was my new prized possession – a 10-dollar plastic gadget I had just received for Christmas. I had dreamed of owning a camera as long as I could remember. Now I imagined a mob of angry men surrounding me, wrestling my camera away from me, exposing my roll of precious, blurry snapshots. Selfish jerks! They were going to destroy my film just so they could get their souls back.

I wanted to skip dinner that night. Granted, I always wanted to skip dinner, but this was different. In addition to food that was going to kill me, there were now people out there who wanted me dead. What if word had spread through the village? What if they were hunting me?

"You have to eat," my dad said. "Everything will be fine."

"How are the Americans tonight?" the waiter asked as we found our table. He was a friendly, rotund man who had taken a liking to Steve and me over the course of the week.

"Fine," my dad smiled, too polite to mention the oyster incident. "David walked all the way to the medina today!"

My muscles tensed. "Don't tell him that!" I thought. What if the hotel staff had caught wind of the incident? We couldn't let them know it was me. Let them think it was a *different* American eight-year-old with a camera who had committed the crime.

"That's far!" the waiter said to me with an impressed wink.

I smiled nervously. "How far is it?"

"About two kilometers."

I didn't know what a kilometer was. I didn't care.

"Tonight's our last night here," my father said. "We're going home to England tomorrow."

The waiter said he would miss us. He wished us a safe journey.

So he was oblivious. Our flight would depart at four the next afternoon. My plan between now and then was to hide in the hotel, my camera stashed deep in my suitcase where no one would find it.

I made it. I survived the journey to the airport. We left warm and sunny Tunisia and touched down late at night in a rare London snow storm. I finished out my year as a British school boy.

We returned to Maryland the following August. As time passed, my first year abroad began to feel like nothing more than a vivid dream. England became a place that existed only in my mind, too far away to touch. Only I really had been there, and on various excursions around Europe and beyond. I had a shoebox full of photographs to prove it – fuzzy, crooked images of our house in Lewisham, our vacations in Greece and Switzerland, and a market square in Tunisia.

Months later, back in my old bedroom in Bethesda, in the house we had rented out during our year away, I was sifting through my pictures. I came across the medina photo. I suddenly felt nauseous. I was nine years old now, beginning to get it that there were lots of different religions in the world, that people took their beliefs very seriously.

I didn't know if I had really stolen those people's souls, but I didn't want the possibility weighing on my conscience. What if their souls really had been captured on this piece of glossy paper? I had a hard time buying that concept – and to this day, I have never been able to ascertain what the real problem was with the photo. What I did understand with clarity, even at age nine, was that the people in the picture did not want to be there. They didn't want to be held in my hand like a souvenir. They weren't a trinket meant to be used for bragging rights on the other side of the planet. I needed to liberate them.

I didn't know the protocol for returning a person's soul if it had been inadvertently captured. What I wanted to do was return the picture to the people I had photographed, but that was impossible. Should I destroy it instead? Would that free their souls or destroy them? I wasn't sure, but keeping the photo felt wrong.

Burning the picture seemed like the way to go. Maybe the smoke would rise into the ether, wherever souls were supposed to hang out. But I wasn't allowed to have bonfires in my bedroom. So on a quiet Saturday afternoon, I came up with the best solution my nine-year-old mind could muster. I sliced the photograph into slivers so thin, the people could never be recognized. With a pair of scissors, I set them free.

PART II

NORWEGIAN 'HOOD

1986-1987

Back in America, I no longer felt like a normal American. I became obsessed with all things foreign. I had dreams at night of discovering a secret shortcut – a ten-minute walk from Bethesda back to Lewisham.

But there was no shortcut. There was a sprawling ocean with waves and sharks and other pesky obstacles. A plane ticket was out of reach on my 35-cents-a-week allowance. In order to afford a trip back to Europe, I would have to rob a bank, but my Gnome Ranger pistol had been lost in the move.

So for the next nine years, I did all I could to create a foreign world around me. At school, I befriended the foreign kids. In suburban Washington, DC, there were many. Some were children of ambassadors, diplomats, or World Bank employees. Others were refugees who had fled wars and poverty in their homelands. They all had stories to tell.

As I got older, I listened to shortwave radio broadcasts on an Army surplus receiver my grandfather passed on to me. By age 11, I was getting my news from the British Broadcasting Corporation, and enduring painfully boring propaganda on Radio Moscow, just because it seemed exotic. Four years later, I got my ham radio license so I could talk to people around the globe. I became a hard core radio nerd. While my friends were out getting into the rite-of-passage trouble most American teens get into, I was holed up in my bedroom, tapping out Morse code to strangers on the other side of the planet.

To counter the nerdy radio stigma, I embraced the British new wave scene. I listened to obscure bands with rebellious haircuts whose records had to be imported. I read British rock magazines. I placed an ad in one, seeking pen pals. I received more than a thousand letters, some from countries I had never heard of.

Through letters and staticky radio signals, I was connecting with people in other countries, but I was also withdrawing from my American reality. By my last year of high school, I'd become a loner, avoiding all senior activities and plotting my escape. In 1986, I finally returned to the world I dreamed of living in – a world where I allowed myself to be different from everybody else, because my passport said I was different.

CONFESSIONS OF A
TEENAGED SMUGGLER

USA - FINLAND - NORWAY

I was off to Norway, back in the days when they'd let you take a baseball bat through airport security.

My bat was at home, in a safe place where it couldn't hurt anybody. But another passenger on the same flight from Washington, DC, to New York had his bat with him. He also appeared to have a lot of drugs with him – not hidden in pockets or a travel bag, but concealed in a much more stealthy place – his bloodstream. The man paced around the airport, murmuring things I suppose one had to be intensely stoned to understand. The handle of his bat peeked out of his duffel bag.

In the 1980s, airport security went something like this: You'd check in for your flight, and they would say, "Mr. Fox, do you have anything in your possession that could be used to bring down an airplane? Knives, guns, cassettes by the J. Geils Band?"

You, the hypothetical passenger and/or terrorist, would chuckle, "Nope, not me." Then the ticket agent would thank you for your honesty and send you and your baseball bat to the security line, where uniformed high school drop-outs working for minimum wage would tell you to please proceed, if they had the necessary English skills to do so.

travel accessories

They were more peaceful times, the 1980s. Terrorists were expected to turn themselves in on the honor system.

So my fellow passenger, strung out on a cocktail of interesting substances, or perhaps just one too many baseballs to the left side of his skull, made it through security, no problem, and proceeded to wander around, making comments that were completely unintelligible, but which appeared, based on his surly expression, to be of menacing intent.

I tried to ignore him. I had just said goodbye to my parents and brother and was officially on my own in the world for the first time. If I was going to die, I told myself, it was going to happen in a more exotic locale than at the airport, trying to get out of town.

I had a long night ahead: an hour-long hop to New York, an overnight flight to Helsinki, Finland, and then a U-turn that would deposit me in Oslo, 25 miles north of the Norwegian fjordside village where I would spend the next year. A 20-minute delay was announced. Then there was a commotion. Then I saw five police officers escorting my all-American baseball-and-LSD-loving co-passenger out of the terminal. Five minutes later, there was an announcement. My flight to New York was canceled due to a "mechanical problem."

PanAm instructed us to catch the Eastern Airlines shuttle in an hour. We'd land at LaGuardia Airport and catch buses to Kennedy with plenty of time to make my 9 p.m. Helsinki flight.

Then the storm blew in. Thunder. Lightning. Hailstones the size of guinea pigs. The airport was closed.

I was an uptight teenager. Worrying was my hobby, but for once I was unusually calm. I had said goodbye to my family. I didn't want to go home to Bethesda and replay the goodbye drama the next day. I tried to just let things fall into place. I was on an adventure.

Five hours later, my adventure had still not left the runway in Washington. We had been told to get off the plane, back on the plane, off the plane again, back on the plane – three times in all. There was no food. Hunger was turning to surliness in some passengers, who were yelling at the flight attendants to quit standing around and DO SOMETHING about the thunder and lightning and gale-force winds.

Finally at 11 p.m., we landed in New York. We were met by a PanAm agent who told us all flights from Kennedy had left for the night. I would later learn this wasn't true. The Helsinki flight I was scheduled on was delayed until 2:30 a.m., but it was cheaper for PanAm to stick me in the same scummy hotel as the other stranded passengers than to transport me alone across town. So they offered me a room, which I was to share with an Iranian lawyer named Joe.

Joe was a pudgy man with a deep voice and hairy back. I guessed he was in his mid to late 40s. Looking back, I have to wonder: Did they do the same cursory screening here as they did at the security checkpoint before deciding to room a 17-year-old boy with an unknown man on his way out of the country?

"Sir, have you ever molested or been tempted to molest a teenage boy? No? How wonderful! Here's your roommate. His name is David Fox. He's young and naïve, so please take good care of him."

Fortunately, though, Joe was an okay guy. We stayed up till 3 a.m., chatting and watching *M*A*S*H*.

The next afternoon, one of the escorts from the exchange program found me at the airport. "Dave," she said, "I'm glad to finally meet you. We were worried about you yesterday."

"I was worried about me yesterday too."

She assured me everything was taken care of. I was rebooked on a flight the next day to Oslo. I'd just have to endure a seven-hour stopover in Helsinki.

Over the next few hours, 90 other kids showed up. Most were headed to Sweden for the year. Eleven were going to Finland. I was one of two Norwegian outcasts.

In Helsinki the next morning, a woman named Tiina met us

at the airport and got the Sweden-bound students onto their connecting flight. She was left with the 11 Finnish students, plus me and Lisa, the other student headed for Norway who had missed the same flight as me the day before. Tiina looked at the two of us, not quite sure what to do.

"We're taking the other students to the language camp," she said. "If you'd like, you could come with us, and I can bring you back here in the afternoon. There's no sense in sitting around the airport for seven hours."

I eyed Tiina skeptically. "Are you sure you'll get us back in time? I don't want to miss another flight."

She promised.

Lisa thought it was a great idea. I wasn't so sure, but I tried to convince myself seeing a bit of Finland, even through my jetlagged haze, would be a nice bonus. So we started toward the customs checkpoint. That's when I stopped Tiina.

"I can't do this," I said. "I'm not legally allowed to enter Finland."

The problem wasn't me entering Finland. The problem was me entering Finland with my ham radio transmitter. My amateur radio station had become my security blanket. For several years, it had satisfied my cravings for contact with foreign cultures. Never mind that soon, I'd be experiencing more foreign culture than I knew what to do with just by getting out of bed each morning. I had insisted on lugging the whole damn station to Norway.

Most countries require a license to operate a shortwave radio transmitter, and importing such equipment without permission is illegal. I had taken care of the paperwork for Norway, but I hadn't anticipated this stop in Finland. My radio wasn't allowed into the country, and there was no place in the airport to stash it without clearing customs first.

Tiina looked at my bag. "It's just a radio, right? They probably won't even know what it is."

Honest, I thought it was a baseball bat!

44

I explained that yes, she was probably right, but they could confiscate it if they did catch me bringing it in illegally.

"Well, here's what we'll do then," Tiina suggested. "You go through customs in front of me. If they stop you, I'll explain the situation, and maybe they'll be okay with it. If not, you'll just have to stay here, but it's worth a try."

I wasn't accustomed to breaking the law. Not in America, at least, but I was starting a new chapter in life. I needed to quit worrying so much. So I put my bag on the X-ray belt. They waved me through, no problem. Officially in the country now, we found a locker for my bag and hopped in one of four cars convoying students out to their language camp.

Soon we were cruising through a lush forest of birch trees. This was a moment I had anticipated – that first sense of having arrived in a very different place. More than the obvious and expected differences, like the language or currency, little things jumped out at me – road signs, license plates, even the lines painted on the roads. Everything looked just a little bit different.

The students staying in Finland structured their arrival differently from the Norwegian program. They had their language camp right away – at a real camp, a spot in the countryside with cabins, a lake, and a sauna. They'd meet their host families in two weeks. In Norway, our host families would be waiting at the airport to take us home. Our "camp" would be at a school in Oslo four weeks later.

We sat outside and introduced ourselves. Welcoming us were some Finnish teenagers who had just returned from a year in the US or Canada. They cracked jokes about how impossible their language was. They laughed when the Americans tried to pronounce their host families' names. The American students looked discouraged.

Tiina drove us back to the airport. She wished us luck and dropped us off at the curb.

"Damn," I said to Lisa as Tiina's car vanished into traffic. "What am I going to do now if they ask about my radio?"

Lisa laughed. "You worry a lot, don't you Dave?"

We went to the security line. "Just be cool," I told myself. Running through my head, however, was the scene from *Midnight Express* when the American gets caught with several pounds of hashish taped to his body and gets the crap beaten out of him in one of Istanbul's notorious prisons. I wondered what the jails were like in Helsinki.

Lisa went first. She made it through, no problem. I set my bag on the X-ray belt.

The man watching the screen stopped the belt as my bag went through. He stared at it for a moment. I was beginning to sweat.

"Don't sweat," I thought. "That's what the guy in *Midnight Express* did and they nailed him!" The belt began moving again. I thought I was clear. I sighed with relief as I reached for my bag.

An officer stopped me. "Wait please," he said to me in English.

Then he switched to Finnish. He called another officer over – a young guy in his early 20s – and spoke to him for a moment.

"Do you speak English?" the younger officer asked me.

"Yes."

"Please come with me."

I looked around for Lisa, but she had already passed through the labyrinth of security barriers.

The man escorted me to a room the size of a small shower. There was barely space for both of us.

"Please open your bag," he instructed.

I obeyed. My hands were shaking, which I knew would only help incriminate me, but I couldn't stop them. A radio commercial I had heard in Maryland, urging Americans not to smuggle drugs, started playing in my head. "It's a bummer to get busted abroad," said a college-aged female who boiled into a 30-second sound bite her tale of incarceration in "a filthy hole" in some unnamed foreign land.

I unzipped my bag. The customs officer took my radio out.

"What is this?" he asked.

"It's a radio," I said, trying to be vague.

"A radio?" The man eyed me. He scrunched his eyebrows. "It's very fancy."

"It's a shortwave radio," I said, hoping he wouldn't notice it could transmit. The microphone that plugged into the front was packed in my suitcase. As long as he thought my radio was just a receiver, I'd be fine.

"What does it do?" he asked.

"Ummm..." I shrugged, "it's a shortwave radio."

He picked up my radio and squinted through the air vent. "Can you open it up?"

"Sure," I said. "Do you have a screwdriver?"

"No." He sounded suspicious. "You don't have something to open it with?"

"I don't carry a screwdriver with me," I said. "If you can get one, I can open it."

He slid the radio off to the side, out of my reach. "Okay. I will have to go find one. But we finish here first." He reached in my bag and pulled out my journal.

I had been keeping a diary for more than a year in anticipation of my time abroad. I had been writing monthly updates of my plans. The officer opened it up and started reading.

"That's my diary," I said, hoping he'd realize it was personal.

"Hmmm," he said, and kept reading.

He was leafing through the first few pages, the pages where I had journaled about choosing which country to go to. Finland had been on my list at one time. I had ruled it out because books about Finnish society warned that the Finns were "reserved people" who "tended to keep to themselves," that they spoke an incredibly complex language, unrelated to all Indo-European languages. I had read about these "reserved people" and written my own teenage interpretation in my diary: "Finland is out because I hear they're really hostile over there."

It struck me now that this was not exactly an open-minded interpretation of a country I'd never set foot in, nor was it a good thing to write before passing through their immigration. But the officer grew bored of my diary and set it aside.

Next he found my Walkman, and a case of tapes. He opened the tape case and started scrutinizing them. He pulled out *Murmur* by REM.

In 1986, REM was still a relatively unknown band with noisy guitars and unintelligible vocals. They were starting to gain headway in the college radio market, but mainstream radio had not yet made them the rock and roll icons they are today.

I had grown tired of mainstream radio. My musical tastes were on the alternative fringes of rock. This was one of the only things that rescued my reputation in American high school as a violin playing, ham radio operating nerd with glasses and a heavy backpack. My obsessions with bands like the Alarm, Icicle Works, and Echo and the Bunnymen gained me at least some limited access into the punk-goth-wannabe crowd.

Now this customs officer, whose job was to save Finland from drug traffickers and spies, was scrutinizing my music collection.

He pulled out a tape by Billy Bragg: *Life's a Riot Between the Wars*. Billy Bragg was a sort of folk-punk hybrid who got his start busking on the streets of London. Against the backdrop of a solitary, distorted electric guitar, he sang songs about left-wing politics and the struggles of the working class.

The customs agent glanced at me from behind the tape case.

This wasn't looking good. It suddenly occurred to me I was an American who had just imported illegal radio equipment into a country that, I had been reminded at the language camp, shared a long and paranoid border with the Soviet Union.

"But officer, I swear to you I am just a dork with weird taste in music!" I wanted to fall to my knees and beg for leniency, but I kept my mouth shut.

Another tape came out of the case. *Neither Washington Nor Mos-*

cow by the Redskins, a jazzy sort of punk band that preached international socialism.

When I packed, lyrics and politics had never crossed my mind. Of my collection of more than 200 cassettes, the ten I chose for the airplane included two that were about to incriminate me as an enemy of Finnish democracy. Why, oh why, couldn't I just listen to Journey and REO Speedwagon like a normal American teenager?

Finally, after a long perusal of my tape collection, the customs agent glanced down at my passport on the desk and spoke to me.

"You're American?" he asked, raising an eyebrow.

"Yes."

The officer smiled. "I like your music!"

Was this a trick?

"I think this is not normal music for an American to listen to."

"Not really," I said. "But I don't like our radio stations. Everything sounds the same."

"Yes!" His smile widened. "We have the same problem in Finland! Always the same shit!"

His profanity caught me off guard. This guy was representing the government of Finland, protecting his nation from smugglers. He was chatting with me now like we were old pals.

"But where do you find this music in America if it is not on the radio?" he asked.

I told him I read British music magazines, or got recommendations from friends. He seemed to be warming up to me. Was my taste in music about to save me from 10 years of hard labor? I decided to run with it.

"Do you have any Finnish bands you like?" I asked.

"Yes but they sing in Finnish."

"That's okay," I said.

He scribbled a few names on a scrap of paper and handed it to me. Then, he began fumbling with my bag, trying to zip my spy radio back inside. "I am sorry to bother you," he said. "I have to. It is my job."

I told him I understood. He was just looking out for my radio-smuggling safety.

"What happened to you?" Lisa asked when I finally emerged into the no-man's-land part of the airport beyond immigration. She looked horrified.

"They strip searched me," I said.

"What?!"

"Just kidding."

Two hours later, I was sound asleep. I had dozed off in my aisle seat as my final flight flew westward. Lisa rattled my shoulder and pointed out the window. "Dave, look!" she said.

I didn't want to look. I wanted to sleep. I took a quick glance to be polite and found my eyes riveted and awake.

Sprawled out below was Oslofjord. It was spectacular – glistening in the late afternoon sun, freckled with sailboats that bobbed and glided between the islands. The houses were made of wood, painted white or maroon or mustard. They rested stoically atop patches of rock scraped bare by centuries of weather.

I was about to descend into one of the planet's northernmost capitals. The faraway-ness started to hit me. I had escaped the land of baseball bats.

A SORT OF HOMECOMING

DRØBAK, NORWAY

Røbak was an idyllic village – almost too quaint to be real. It hugged the shores of Oslofjord, with a harbor for a couple of hundred sailboats and a never-ending symphony of squawking gulls. Paths along the shoreline meandered through gray, rocky outcroppings where the land had been scraped bare in the last Ice Age. Uphill from the water, a cozy town square boasted a supermarket, a post office, a bank, a record shop, and a theater that showed movies a few nights a week – usually subtitled American films the Oslo cinemas were done with. A single road led out of town, into farmland that seemed detached from the seafaring town center.

I knocked on the door to my new home. Marius answered and shook my hand. "No Woman, No Cry" was wailing from upstairs – loud enough to wake Bob Marley in his grave. A young, blonde-haired girl sat on the entryway floor. A short, pudgy guy peeked from the stairs, laughing.

"This is my sister Hanne and my brother Thomas," Marius said. "Thomas doesn't speak English. Hanne speaks a little."

"No I don't," Hanne said, grimacing. She was 11. Thomas was 19. Marius was the same age as me.

I'd been in Norway for four days, living with a temporary host family until my family for the year returned from vacation. Marius, Thomas, and Hanne were my new siblings. My Norwegian "parents," Per and Tordis, would be on their sailboat for a few more days, but Marius had invited me to come meet the younger generation in the family.

More people crowded the entryway of the house to check me out. Marius continued with the introductions. "This is my girlfriend Anne, and my friends Ronny and Tor-Erik and Tom-William and Vibeke." Most of them were slugging down beer or wine. I had come to meet my new host family and stumbled upon a frat party.

"Hey man! How's it goin'?" Tor-Erik stepped forward and shouted over Mr. Marley. Tor was a lanky guy with curly hair. He tried unsuccessfully to speak with an American accent, laughing at his own English and swigging his beer.

The house was built into the side of a steep hill. Giant boulders like the ones on the beach protruded right into the downstairs bathroom. It was a plot of land most Americans wouldn't think of building on, but Norwegians had a knack for working with nature, welcoming it into their homes rather than jackhammering it away.

We climbed the stairs to the living room. Empty bottles cluttered the hardwood floors. "That's my sister's room," Marius said, turning the music down. "And that's our garden."

The garden had a sprawling view over Oslofjord. The kitchen and dining room floor, and even the dining room walls, were made of stone. Up another steep staircase was a parlor and the master bedroom. A balcony offered an even better view of the water.

"We are going to go waterskiing," Marius said. "It is at a place called Kjærnes. Do you want to come with us? You can borrow a bathing costume."

I had never waterskied in my life. I swam with the coordination of a Golden Retriever. A friend in America had once warned me that when you learn to waterski, water finds its way into orifices not intended for taking in water. Furthermore, I was still jetlagged and culture shocked. Did I want to strap planks of wood to my feet and have a motor boat drag me through arctic waters at high speeds while a group of strangers commented on my performance in a language I couldn't understand? Oh, yes please.

My impending death in the fjord was not my biggest problem, however. I was also painfully shy, and terrified these people were going to quickly discover the secret that I was uncool. Growing up in the suburbs of the world's most powerful city had taken a toll on my sense of self-worth. Bethesda, Maryland, boasted the best public high school in the country when it came to academics, but socially, the place was a battleground of cliques, none of which I ever clicked with.

These people were out of my league. They cranked reggae and partied while their parents were away. It wasn't going to take them long to uncover my dirty little secret that I was an introverted, socially inept dork who was terrified of people and even more deathly afraid of getting into trouble.

"Sure," I said. "I've never waterskied before. Let's go!"

We piled into the family's bright green Lada – a Soviet-made car about the same size as my suitcase. Those who didn't fit in the Lada were following behind with Ronny, who was driving his parents' car.

I was in the back seat, sandwiched between Marius and Tor-Erik. Tor-Erik laughed. "It's a Russian car, man! What do you think about *that*?"

He seemed to anticipate a frightened reaction. I was an American in a vehicle from the so-called "Evil Empire." What was he expecting me to do? Check the seat cushions for microphones?

I shrugged. "Ummm, I don't know."

"My parents don't like to buy expensive cars," Marius said, almost apologetically, as Thomas sped uphill toward the highway. "They spend their money on other things like their boat."

"What kind of car do you got in America, man?" Tor asked.

"Ummm, my dad has a Toyota, and my mom drives a Chevy Concourse."

"A what?"

"A Chevrolet."

"Wow man! A Chevrolet!" Tor's eyes grew wider.

"Yeah."

"Everybody in America has big cars. That's my dream, to own an American car."

Tor reached into a bag. He pulled out a bottle of beer and a cigarette lighter. "You want a beer?"

Here it was – the moment of truth.

I drank beer in the States, but only with the utmost of discretion, when there was no risk of getting busted. Once I reached high school, I discovered an added bonus of having friends from other countries. Some of them came from places with no drinking age. Their parents would buy a case of beer and drink a couple of them. A week later, the case would be mysteriously gone. No questions were ever asked.

So in theory, I had no objection to having a beer or six, but I was under strict instructions from my exchange program. Certain offenses – murder, arson, and underage drinking, would get me a ticket on the first flight back to America. No jury. No trial. No second chances. To make matters worse, we were in a car. Drinking in a moving vehicle is legal in Norway as long as you aren't the driver, but to me, it seemed akin not only to murder, but to eating the bodies afterward.

"I'm not 18 yet," I said, squirming.

"Neither are we," Marius said.

"Marius have the best parents in the world!" Vibeke shouted from the front passenger seat.

"My parents tell us to be responsible, and not drink too much, and telephone if we get a problem," Marius said. "Thomas is not drinking because he is driving."

"Well," I explained, "they can send me back to America if I drink alcohol."

"That's okay," Marius said. "You don't like to drink beer?"

"Ummm, no. I mean yes. I like to drink beer. But I can't."

"Just take it cool maaannn!!" Tor shouted and he slapped me on the back. He handed me his bottle and retrieved another from his bag, popping off the bottle cap with his cigarette lighter. "Cheerio!" He laughed again and slapped me on the back a second time.

"Don't worry," Marius said, smiling. "If you don't want to drink it, I take it myself, but if you want to drink, it's just no problem."

I eyed the bottle. I scanned outside the window for cops. I was being uncool. Did I want to follow the rules or did I want to experience life as a normal Norwegian teenager? I took a swig.

"Wow," I said. "That's a really good beer."

American teenagers drank what they could get. Quality microbrews weren't a consideration.

"Wow man!" Tor mimicked. "That's cool man!" He laughed again.

"It is a Norwegian beer," Marius said. "From a *bryggeri* in Oslo. It is a very good beer."

I was suddenly feeling emboldened. "*Skål*," I said, raising my bottle.

The car exploded with a cry of approval. "You are learning Norwegian!" Vibeke said.

I smiled shyly. "The important words."

"I like you, Dave," Tor-Erik said. "You're cool, man."

"You're cool too," I said. "*Skål*."

Marius toasted me too. Vibeke looked back from the front seat and smiled. Thomas said something about me in Norwegian. He seemed sufficiently impressed with my language skills.

We screeched into a gravel lot. A small motor boat bobbed in the water.

Thomas was the designated driver on land and sea. He spoke no English, but he managed to communicate nonetheless. He gestured to me: "Would you like to put on a lifejacket and get dragged through the water until I look back and notice you choking?"

I looked at Marius to interpret. "I'm pretty tired today," I said. "Maybe I'll just watch."

Tor-Erik handed me another beer.

A few hours and a few beers later, we were back at the house. I was starting to relax. Thomas had gone on a mission to the grocery store across the street. He was working to catch up now that his designated driver shift was over.

I was doing my best to encourage him – and everybody else. I was teaching them to play quarters – a drinking game that involved bouncing a coin into a glass and then designating who was to drink. Hanne was playing with cola. Her sobriety gave her the upper hand against the rest of us. My 11-year-old host-sister, whom I had met just hours earlier, was taking great pride in getting me sloshed.

My confidence boosted by the alcohol, I had also taken over the stereo. My punk-jazz-Socialist tape by the Redskins was a hit. The living room became a mosh pit as the band tried to incite a riot with tunes like "Kick Over the Statues."

I don't think anyone else was catching the lyrics. And for me, a shy, too-polite, suburban boy, it was an unlikely musical choice. But I related to the music in a weird way. I needed to incite my own revolution – not against the evil Capitalist bourgeoisie, but against my own perceptions of myself. The Redskins sang about oppression of the working class. I was living with my own oppression of myself. For years, I had been tiptoeing around, apologizing for who I was, playing over and over in my head a tape that told me I wasn't cool enough.

I had just moved away from everyone and everything I knew. I wasn't realizing it yet, but running away from home in the socially acceptable manner of becoming an exchange student was giving me the opportunity to reinvent myself. I hadn't just come to a foreign country; I'd come to a foreign place in my mind as well. I had just pulled off my first test. I felt like I had tricked everyone into believing I knew how to fit in. It hadn't yet occurred to me maybe I really *was* fitting in.

LEARNING TO TALK

OSLO AND DRØBAK, NORWAY

K nut Bø had pain in the teeth. He was on visit at the house of the tooth-doctor.

"I am called Knut Bø," said Knut Bø to the tooth-doctor.

"It is pleasant to meet you," said the tooth-doctor. "What is in the way?"

"I have pain in the teeth. I live in Oslo. I work as carpenter."

We were riveted to the story – all 22 of us – a group of American and Canadian teenagers, taking great delight in deciphering the personal lives of poorly drawn cartoons in our Norwegian text. In our heads, we were translating the dialogues, word for word, and understanding for the first time why foreigners spoke English with such screwed up grammar. They couldn't help it. Somebody had rearranged all the words from the places they were supposed to be in the sentences. Along with this new-found sympathy for non-native English speakers came the horror that we were saying really stupid things in Norwegian.

With our limited new vocabulary, we were amusing ourselves with the most idiotic of sentences. Every few minutes, Lisa would lean over to me. "Hey, Dave," she would whisper, *"Spiser mye grønnsaker!"*

"Eats much vegetables!" she was demanding, with grammar only a recently-landed foreigner could get away with. Then she would laugh, and I would laugh, and the teacher would toss us an annoyed glance that said, "Pay attention."

When you've been living in a foreign country for a month, unable to understand a single word, and you suddenly learn the word for vegetables is *grønnsaker* (literally translated: "green things"), you find yourself filled with a linguistic giddiness that makes you giggle about broccoli.

Our teacher was a guy named Trygve. He was chubby, with a bushy mustache, droopy cheeks, and a calm seriousness about him. He wasn't particularly cool, but we idolized him anyway. Seven hours a day for two weeks, his job was to explain the idiosyncrasies of Norwegian and make us fluent.

We were learning that in Norwegian, "Will you marry me?" and "Will you poison me?" are the same question, with only a subtle grammatical difference to distinguish the two. Trygve bestowed us with other useful information, such as, "Hose and snake are the same word in Norwegian," and, "In Norway, we call a dentist a *tannlege,* which means, 'tooth-doctor.' Now please turn to page 43 and read about Knut Bø."

The language situation in my new household varied from person to person. Marius spoke the imperfect but basically fluent English of most Norwegian 18-year-olds. My host-father, Per, was an engineer, and used English in his job. Thomas had forgotten English as soon as he finished high school, but he was a genius when it came to improvised sign language. Hanne, at age 11, had been studying for three years, but was too shy to speak to me. Tordis, my Norwegian mother, was also timid. She knew more than she realized. She apologized frequently in English for not knowing how to speak English.

Somehow, we all communicated. When communication broke down, Bill Cosby would reunite us.

Cosby med familie – *The Cosby Show* to American audiences – came on after dinner every Tuesday. The comedy about the Huxtable family was one of many American TV shows purchased by Norwegian state television because buying programs from America and subtitling them was cheaper than producing original shows for the relatively small Norwegian audience. Norwegians would read the translated dialogue. So would I, pausing frequently to look up words in my dictionary that I had just looked up and forgotten three minutes earlier. And seven minutes earlier. And 12 minutes earlier. It was a tedious process, but one word at a time, things were falling into place.

On the first day of school, I hadn't understood a single word. For seven hours, I had sat through history, religion, social studies, and Norwegian literature.

Freaked out by the thought of hours of classes every day in a language I did not yet understand, I came up with the brilliant idea that one of my elective subjects should be French. I had taken two high school years of French in the US. In French class, I could kind of understand what was going on – better than I was understanding the history of Norway in Norwegian. But after class, I would emerge into the hallway muttering a baffling mixture of *norsk* and *français*. My French teacher saw what was happening one day, and politely suggested that I leave his classroom and never come back.

I was making friends at school – more easily than I made friends in America, in spite of the language barrier. Or maybe it was because of the language barrier. My schoolmates had spent 10 years of their lives learning useless English phrases. They were tired of reading about John Smith, the carpenter who had to go to the dentist because he had a toothache. They were tired of asking to pass the vegetables. They wanted to speak real English. Useful English. The English of MTV. My job, as far as they were concerned, was to be their monolingual mascot, never learning their language, because if I did learn their language, they could no longer show off their extensive knowledge of American obscenities.

Conflicts resulted. I really wanted to learn Norwegian, and I knew the only way to learn it was to speak it. But they weren't letting me, even for the most basic of phrases.

"*Unnskyld,*" I would say – "Excuse me" – summoning every ounce of Norwegian in my brain. "*Hvor er toalettet?*"

"Oh, the toilet?" came the reply in English. "Cool, man. You're the American, right? It's down the stairs on the left. Take my hand, and we'll make it. I swear."

"Huh?"

"You know. *'Take my hand, and we'll make it, I swear. Whoa-OH! Livin' on a prayer!'* It's Bon Jovi. They're the best band in America. Don't you know them?"

"Oh. Ummm, thanks."

Conversations like this would sometimes be accompanied by air guitar or gratuitous butt-wiggling. I would slither away, wishing I had moved to Uzbekistan instead, where I wouldn't have to face a barrage of exported American pop culture.

I arrived in Norway in August. According to literature from my exchange program, I would have near fluent comprehension by Christmas, *if* I worked hard enough. And I *was* working hard, doing all I could to absorb everything. I never went anywhere without my dictionary. I was constantly putting my fork down at the dinner table, or stepping away from group conversations at parties, or interrupting my train of thought in class, or pausing before entering the bank, to look up a word I might need.

My brain was beginning to fry.

I was exhausted. It wasn't just the constant linguistic bombardment. I was adjusting to a new school, a family very different from my American family, a foreign diet, not to mention the usual hormonal hell adolescents – especially shy adolescents – go through. On top of that, winter was coming to northern Europe. The sun was rising later and setting earlier every day, until eventually, daylight did not start until the second hour of school and darkness had fallen by the time I returned home at 3:30. I began sleeping 10 or 11 hours a night. Tordis was convinced I was ill.

"There is a disease that makes you very tired," she said. "You must see a doctor."

"You mean mono? I don't have mono."

"Yes. I think you do."

But I knew I didn't. I had already contracted the so-called kissing disease in eighth grade, in the most humiliating of ways, probably sharing a water bottle at Boy Scout camp.

"I've had it before," I said. "And you can only get it once."

"I still think you should see a doctor."

I wasn't going to see a doctor. No way. I remembered the blood test several years earlier when I was diagnosed with mono. My doctor had jabbed me with the world's largest needle, specially designed to inflict extra pain. He had wriggled it into my vein and held it there while his hand trembled like a jackhammer. I think he might have been in the early stages of Parkinson's Disease. He was in no condition to be giving blood tests. I wasn't going through that again.

"I'm fine," I said to Tordis. "My brain's just overloaded."

She was skeptical until a couple of weeks later when a letter arrived. It was a letter from the exchange program, explaining that this was the part of the year when many exchange students began staring into space and drooling uncontrollably.

"This is a normal part of the adjustment process," the letter said, mentioning parenthetically at the end that when learning a new language through total immersion, two extra hours of sleep per night were necessary in order to avoid complete mental collapse.

I felt constantly exhausted, but my hard work was beginning to pay off. Three months into my stay, I was understanding enough Norwegian to figure out that Knut Bø really needed to get a life. And perhaps begin flossing.

The letter contained exciting news as well. To give us a break from cultural overload in Norway, we were going on a trip to the so-called "Evil Empire." It was time for a communist party in Leningrad.

COMMUNIST PARTYING

LENINGRAD, USSR

W e had strict instructions from our exchange program about how to behave when we reached the Soviet border. We were not to bring in any magazines, newspapers, or cassette tapes. If we did, border guards could detain us for hours in an effort to censor Western propaganda. Cameras were allowed, but film might be confiscated. We were not to take pictures until we reached Leningrad, not to joke about bombs or spying, not to argue with the soldiers, not to hiccup, breathe, blink, burp, or attempt to order a cheeseburger. When you enter enemy territory, it's important to be on your best behavior.

Growing up in Cold War America, I had learned a thing or two about life in the USSR. The Soviet Union was a powerful nation with a government that punished anyone who engaged in sordid capitalist activities. Anybody caught with a black market copy of Michael Jackson's *Thriller* album, for example, could be shipped off to a Siberian labor camp. That, I thought, was excellent domestic policy; however, my high school teachers, most of whom had crappy taste in music, tried to explain to me this was a flagrant human rights violation.

The USSR, I was taught, was a country where nobody smiled, and everything was bleak and gray. Spies prowled the streets. Telephones were bugged. They had nuclear weapons that could disintegrate millions of innocent Americans at the push of a button.

That last part, about the button, the Soviets admitted to. They could theoretically liquidate all 240-million of our capitalist butts in a heartbeat if they wanted, but they promised they wouldn't as long as we didn't zap them either. They were spending a gigantic portion of their national budget on nuclear weapons for the same reason we were: to guarantee peace. If both sides had weapons of the same strength, nobody was going to fire the first shot. They promised. We promised. But nobody trusted the other side.

In October, 1986, Ronald Reagan and Mikhail Gorbachev held historic peace talks in Iceland, but the summit ended in a stalemate and embarrassment for both leaders. Our nations were like two snarling pit bulls, circling each other, baring teeth, never going in for the kill, but not willing to let down their guard either.

The posturing frightened me. Buying bombs, big bombs, bombs that could obliterate half the planet with one push of "the button," didn't strike me as a good route toward world peace. I thought maybe a big international party – please check your nuclearware at the door – would be a better idea. Now, less than a month after the Iceland summit, I was about to enter the land President Reagan called the "Evil Empire."

Honest, it is my baseball bat

Marius and I chugged out of Oslo's central train station one morning with a handful of other exchange students. A November chill filled the air and sunrise seemed tardy. A pre-dawn glow muffled the city's outline. By late morning, the first feeble rays of direct light flickered on the horizon as we crossed into Sweden. By mid-afternoon, we were in Stockholm where we met several dozen more exchange students and host siblings. We boarded an overnight ship to Helsinki. There were 108 of us – mostly Americans, with a handful of Canadians and Scandinavians – all hyperactive teenagers, all indoctrinated in one way or another with spooky Cold War stereotypes of what life in the Soviet Union was like.

When we reached Helsinki the next day, we drove eastward to the Finnish-Soviet frontier. Finnish soldiers checked our passports and waved us onward, into a desolate no-man's land that separated West from East. I couldn't help but feel a sense of awe and fear. The mood on the bus grew somber.

Gianni was our tour guide. He came from Italy, but he spoke fluent English, Swedish, Finnish, and Russian. He explained what was going on in the forest around us as we neared the Soviet checkpoint.

"Customs is just a couple of minutes up the road," he said. "We can't stop the bus between here and there. They're watching us right now. These trees around us have cameras hidden in them. There are snipers in the woods. You can't see them, but if we were to stop the bus or pull off to the side for any reason, they'd surround us very fast and we could be in a lot of trouble."

Up to this point, Gianni had been a fun, laid-back guy, but now, he spoke in a knowing whisper, as if anything louder might be intercepted on a monitoring device.

"They will search the bus when we get to the checkpoint," he continued. "Sometimes it takes 20 minutes. Sometimes it takes two hours. Remember, no photographs and no talking when they come on the bus."

This was creepy. The tension was palpable. I was tightening all of my own muscles, and on top of that, a collective nervous energy among all of the students hung in the air.

We rolled through the forest slowly, obeying speed limit signs. This slow crawl along a desolate swatch of highway added to the tension. Then, without warning, on an empty stretch of road obscured by trees, shots rang out.

I froze. A wave of nausea filled my stomach. I slumped down in my seat, scanning through the window for the source of the bullets. Where was the shooting coming from? Were we the target? It sounded as if the shots were firing directly above our heads.

Then I realized – the sound of gunshots really was *directly* above my head, just inches away – coming from the speakers on the bus

PA system. Gianni doubled over with laughter in the front seat. He was making shooting noises with his mouth on the microphone. This wasn't the first time he had crossed into the Soviet Union with a busload of paranoid Americans.

Some of us laughed at Gianni's humor, but we stifled our chuckles as we neared the border. Jokes about getting shot at lose their sparkle when you find yourself rolling toward soldiers with large guns. All we had to do now was pass through customs, and we'd be in – behind the Iron Curtain, in the land of vodka and oppression. After a lifetime of stories about the horrors of Soviet living conditions, actually seeing the mysterious land just feet ahead on the other side of a barricade felt surreal.

"No talking when they enter the bus," Gianni repeated as we rolled to the guard post. We could tell from his voice he was serious now.

First the soldiers inspected the outside of the bus. They had German Shepherds – specially trained, I gathered, to sniff out Michael Jackson tapes. The soldiers looked under the bus with mirrors, scanning for stowaways in the chassis. They opened the gas tank and plunged a dipstick in. Then two of them boarded our bus and started pacing the aisle.

They spoke a familiar-sounding language – a sinister tongue I had heard in spy movies. They squinted at us, as if our group of 15 to 18-year-olds might be plotting to bring down their government. They scavenged in ashtrays and inspected under our seats. They rifled through random bags.

Out of my bag, a soldier pulled a copy of the *Herald Tribune*, a newspaper published in those days under a joint agreement between the *New York Times* and *Washington Post*. I stifled a gasp. I had forgotten to dispose of the paper in Finland. It had a front page article that was not flattering about the Soviets. Was I in trouble?

The soldier looked at my newspaper. Then, to my surprise, he didn't take it away. He just shrugged, and put it back in my bag.

The bus was ghostly silent, except for murmurs between the

Vee haf vays of making you eat borscht!

65

two soldiers. They combed through the bus, staring us down, scrutinizing our passports. Finally, they turned to leave.

As they were exiting the bus, just as we thought we were free to enter the land of no freedom, a loud click shattered the silence.

It was a familiar noise, the unquestionable sound of a camera shutter opening and closing for a sliver of time.

Our pre-tour literature had told us not to take pictures at the border. Gianni had told us not to take pictures at the border. Signs at the border showing cameras with red X's through them reinforced that point. Buses could be detained for hours if one person didn't follow the rules. One of the soldiers was already out the bus door, but the other one heard the click. He spun around, glaring.

He paced through the aisle, waiting for the culprit to confess. He wasn't saying a word. All he did was glower. I was sweating. How long would this go on? How long did we have before the enemy would release the radioactive gas, or the snapping dogs would come corral us into filthy cells?

"*Vee haf vays of makink you talk,*" an imaginary voice whispered in my ear.

The soldier shuffled to the back of the bus, where the click had come from. He couldn't find the photographer. Nobody around her was giving her up. This worried me. If the soldier couldn't figure out whose camera it had come from, he was probably going to confiscate all of our cameras. He turned, and started his slow journey back toward the front, staring each of us down as he went. Every footstep sounded like another tick of a time bomb.

Suddenly, a girl at the back of the bus could no longer stand the silence. A thought in her head escaped through her mouth.

"Hey! He's kind of cute!"

We were like a rubber band, stretched to its limits, and with that comment, we snapped. We couldn't contain ourselves any longer. The bus exploded with laughter.

Tears ran down my face. I doubled over, afraid my ribs would crack from laughing so hard. The soldier turned bright red. He shot suspicious glances around the bus. He could tell we were mocking him, but it suddenly dawned on us that this man who had been sent on board to weed out evil Western propaganda spoke not a word of English. No wonder he gave me my newspaper back.

Fuming, he spun around and left the bus. We laughed harder. I sat up and wiped the tears from my eyes. The bus rolled forward. We were in.

For the next hour, we drove through a bleak landscape of forests and factories. Clunky trucks spewed exhaust. As we neared the city that was then called Leningrad, street signs in the Cyrillic alphabet came into view. The sun was setting by the time we reached our hotel.

In 1986, Intourist was a Soviet government agency designed to assist foreign visitors in finding "appropriate" accommodations with all the modern amenities: toilets, showers, and monitoring devices. If you were an American going to the Soviet Union in those days, odds are you went with an Intourist group. They were the sole supplier of local guides, who were rumored to double as spies, and they ran all the hotels Westerners could stay in.

Our hotel room had a sour odor and phlegm-colored wall paper. A bright red, plastic radio sat on a small table. You could turn the volume down all the way, but there was no off switch. I had heard stories of other travelers turning up their radios and finding themselves privy to conversations of other hotel guests. I threw Marius a knowing glance as I fiddled with the dials. We were being spied upon.

Were we? I tried to do the math. The Hotel Leningrad had about 400 rooms. How many people were they employing to listen to us through our radios? In this land that boasted zero unemployment, did each room come with its own personal spy, or did we have to share our spy with other hotel guests? Did our spy understand English? What about Norwegian? They weren't employing spies for such an obscure language, were they? Where did the spies hang out? Was there a spy room in the hotel basement, or were our conversations being monitored at some underground bunker deep in the forest by chain-smoking goons in trench coats?

I needed to know these things before I broke the law. In spite of my paranoia, a small legal infraction was on my agenda.

There was one small souvenir I wanted to take home – a one-ruble note. Exporting Soviet currency was forbidden, but what were the chances they'd search my front pockets?

Marius and I started unpacking. "Do you think we can get a ruble?" Marius asked in English.

"We're not supposed to do that!" I scolded, pointing to the radio. I grabbed his arm and pulled him into the bathroom. I turned on the shower to muffle our conversation. It was a trick I had learned on TV.

"Marius!" I hissed in broken Norwegian. "Don't talk about smuggling currency! We could be arrested!"

"Calm down, Dave," he said. "They can't be listening to all of us!"

"You never know!"

After dinner, Gianni set us loose. "Just be sure you're back at the hotel by 2 a.m.," he said. "At two, the drawbridges go up and stay up for the night. If you're not back here by then, you'll be stuck out on the street until six."

This freedom to wander surprised me. We were in the land of the Commies. They had searched our bags and bugged our rooms. Were they really going to let us roam their streets unguarded?

It seemed they were. There was nary a spy in sight. Just a curious crowd of eight or nine Soviet teens, who gathered outside the hotel in search of Western contraband – Marlboros, bubble gum, and ballpoint pens.

Before leaving Scandinavia, word had spread through the exchange student grapevine of a black market for these items. Some of us had stocked up on them, and most of us were happy to give away what we had. But one American living in Sweden – I'll call her Karen – was trying to negotiate, charging outrageous prices in US dollars for her stash of clandestine Bubblicious.

"What are you doing?" I interrupted.

Karen started to explain herself. The Russian girl she was negotiating with had a desperate look on her face. The American's prices were high, but she was selling pure, premium quality gum. The good shit.

"You're totally ripping these people off!" I said.

"Yeah, but she said she wanted...."

Ellen, another American living in Sweden, pushed me aside and wrestled the handful of pens and gum from Karen. "Here," she said, thrusting them into the Russian girl's hands. "They're for you."

The Russian girl looked confused.

"They're a gift."

Karen looked dejected. We were ruining her new career as a gum pusher.

We splintered into smaller tribes and prowled the streets. The Volga River ran in front of our hotel. It shimmered, reflecting the dull glow of low-wattage street lamps that sported giant red banners. The architecture on the pre-1917 buildings was grand and majestic, though many of the buildings looked run down.

Marius and I and a few other Americans wandered until midnight. I hadn't noticed Marius had been carrying his blue duffel bag around all night. Alone in the hotel elevator now, he patted the bag's zipper a couple of times and winked.

I raised my eyebrows. He pointed down at his shoes.

He was wearing his brown leather dress shoes now. The falling apart white Nikes he had on when we left the hotel were gone.

I scrunched my eyebrows harder.

He unzipped the bag.

Inside was a Soviet military jacket. While I had been breaking up a bubble gum price gouging scam, Marius had been doing business with a soldier.

"Are you crazy?" I whispered when we got to the room.

"I'm not going to hide it," he answered in English. "That's how you get a problem. I just put it at the top of my bag. If they find it, I give it to them."

The next morning, our Intourist guide's voice droned from the bus's PA system as we drove through the city. She recited a well-rehearsed script about her great nation. I tuned it out. I was far more interested in the exhaust-spewing trucks outside, and the chubby, headscarf-clad ladies who waddled down the street. I wasn't interested in history. I was interested in people. I wanted to tell them I believed in world peace and nuclear arms reduction, even if I was a capitalist pig. I wanted to visit their homes, their schools, their shops. But I wasn't allowed. The only scheduled shopping on our visit was a *Beriozhka* shop that sold incomplete decks of Russian playing cards, and little red CCCP pins, and wooden dolls you could open up to find more wooden dolls inside. The *Beriozhka* shops were the only shops we were allowed to visit. They did not accept Soviet rubles. Only so-called "hard currency." Soviet citizens were not allowed inside.

I had met some real Russians outside our hotel the night before – sort of – but I hadn't really been able to talk to them. None of them spoke English. The *Beriozhka* shops seemed to confirm that the Soviet government didn't want me mingling with its citizens.

"But I'm harmless," I wanted to tell someone. I felt sad.

Our bus tour around the city continued. For lunch, we ate at a hard currency restaurant reserved specially for tourists. I wanted a scruffy neighborhood café. After lunch we had two rushed hours in the sprawling Hermitage art museum. By mid-afternoon, we were driving back to the hotel.

"I have a surprise for you," Gianni said at the end of the tour after our Intourist guide handed over the microphone. "I've talked to some friends here and we've arranged a party in a discotheque tonight where you can meet some Russian teenagers."

A wave of applause rang through the bus. *This* was what I wanted to do all along.

"Now, the hotel where we are staying usually gives you some champagne in your rooms, but they were told not to by your group leader."

The applause was followed by a groan.

"But I had a talk with him and he agreed you can take your champagne to the disco tonight."

A louder wave of applause rang through the bus.

"There's just one thing. You have to hide it. Soviet teenagers aren't allowed to have alcohol in places like this, so please don't let any of them see it."

Was he serious? At our age, we were experts at sneaking alcohol, but did he think 108 teenagers could successfully hide 54 bottles of champagne from another group of teenagers? Besides, keeping our champagne to ourselves seemed like no way to foster world peace.

In the evening, we were bused across town to a cement building with a dance club in the basement. The club was already filled with Soviet teenagers. They eyed us curiously as we entered, probably wondering if all Americans shuffled around nervously with big, bottle-shaped lumps in their jackets. We found seats at tables, and suddenly, the room was divided up like a junior high school dance, only we were separated by governments rather than gender – Westerners on one side, Soviets on the other. I wanted to say hello, but I wasn't going to make the first move. I also wasn't going to be the first one to pull out my bottle.

The tables had glasses of juice on them. It wasn't real juice, but a Tang-like powdered mix; just add water. A few of us sipped our juice and argued over who was going to uncork the first champagne bottle. After a few minutes, John, an exchange student from California, approached our table. He looked nervous.

"We shouldn't be drinking the juice," he said.

"Why not?"

"It might have tap water in it."

71

On the boat to Helsinki, a chaperone had warned us, "Whatever you do, don't drink the tap water. If you do, you will have severe amoebic dysentery for the next six months."

In parts of the Soviet Union, tap water might cause a mildly upset stomach, but Leningrad was special. There was a nasty bacteria strain in the pipes. Residents built up immunities, but our systems weren't used to it. We were warned a single glass of water could land us in the hospital. Now it might be too late, but there was nothing we could do. Other than find something else to drink.

The Soviet kids seemed to be losing interest in us. They weren't scrutinizing us as much now. Maybe we could discreetly open a bottle. I was too inexperienced to know you can't open champagne discreetly. Bottles pop. Corks fly. If you're lucky, nobody loses an eye. Somebody opened a bottle. The cork rocketed across the room.

I looked down at the table, as if I hadn't seen a thing. Clearly this was a bad idea. We needed to put our bottles away before we got in trouble.

Another cork flew.

And another.

Suddenly, the room was like a giant popcorn popper.

Our story was out: We had come bearing booze.

A DJ started spinning records – British and American pop music: Wham, Madonna, and to my horror, Michael Jackson. Minutes later, all the apprehension had left the room and we were all up, dancing.

I pulled Gianni aside. "I thought this sort of music was illegal here," I said.

"You can't buy it in the shops," he explained. "But these are special kids. Their families all have Communist Party connections. They have special privileges. They get more exposure to the West than most Soviet teens."

I was disappointed. A few months earlier, Boomtown Rats lead singer Bob Geldof had organized a series of concerts called Live Aid to raise money for African famine relief. There had been two huge events in London and New York, and smaller concerts in other cities all over the world. There had even been a live satellite feed from Moscow, featuring one of the most popular Soviet rock bands. I wanted to hear Russian rock. Michael Jackson was ruining my cultural experience.

But really, he wasn't. After so many years of hearing how sinister the Soviets were, my suspicion was confirmed – that most of them were really decent people who had the misfortune of living under an oppressive regime. We didn't need to fear each other. We were dancing together now, attempting to communicate, ignoring the fact that we couldn't speak each other's languages. We traded addresses even though we couldn't read each other's alphabets. We smiled. We flirted. For a few hours, we got to be friends with the people we'd been told our entire lives were our enemies.

At 11 p.m., as we all filed out of the building, I tapped my friend Jared on the shoulder. "Reagan and Gorbachev have been doing it all wrong," I said. "They need to quit having so many meetings. They should just get drunk and go out dancing." That, we had just proven, that was the productive way to foster international friendship.

We crossed back into Finland the following afternoon. They waved us through at the border without inspecting anyone's bags. Marius smuggled his military jacket across without a hitch, and I still have the crisp one-ruble note I stashed in my jeans.

Gorbachev and Reagan met again and became friends. They took the first significant steps in thawing the Cold War. At least the first official steps. I like to think our party in the disco that night played a role on a more personal level. Governments like to tell their citizens who their friends and enemies are. All too often, we listen blindly. It's amazing how quickly a glass of champagne, a cup of tea, a family photo, or a shared bar of chocolate can dispel so much mistrust.

Democracy came to Russia a few years later, and the Soviet Union was dissolved. Michael Jackson is no longer banned among common citizens. Other than that, life there has improved.

INTERMISSION

COWERING UNDER MY DESK

Before I go any further, there's a cultural issue I need to address. By "cultural issue," I mean, "Norwegian teenagers drinking lots of booze." We have experienced this phenomenon in previous chapters, and there is more to come.

This is a sensitive topic, I realize. I realize this because as this book was about to go to press, an editor advised me to delete all references to teenage drinking, thereby shortening this section from 56 pages to three-and-a-half pages. She explained that if I told the truth about the sordid behaviors of (a) 97 percent of all Norwegian high school seniors, and (b) myself at age 18, radical American puritans might rise up and launch a massive boycott against this book.

After weeks of labored reflection, I have reached the conclusion that my tales of Norwegian teenage drinking must remain uncensored for two reasons: (1) As a writer of non-fiction, it is my responsibility to tell the truth. (2) Let's face it: A massive boycott of my book by radical American puritans would be pretty gosh darn good for book sales. So seriously, dear puritans, come! Picket outside my home! You are welcome! Don't forget to invite the media! I'll brew coffee!

That having been said, I don't want to sound cavalier about

teenage drinking. There are a couple of things I should explain about Norwegian society:

Most Norwegian teenagers finish high school a year later than American teens. This is not because they are drunk. It's just how their school system works. Norway's drinking age is 18 for beer and wine, 20 for hard liquor. Therefore, most Norwegians can legally drink alcohol before they finish high school. So the chapters you are about to read do not contain any illegal behavior. (Well, except for the vodka.)

We in America have a drinking age of 21 for all alcoholic beverages. This is the highest drinking age in the world. This national drinking age took effect in the 1980s after lawmakers figured out that young adults in states with high drinking ages were driving to states with lower drinking ages, getting sloshed, and then driving home. The results of these excursions were bad. Very bad.

Norway has chosen to combat the drunk driving problem with harsh punishments for driving drunk, instead of harsh punishments for being 18. Their laws work – far better than America's. In Norway, a blood alcohol content of .02 percent is legally drunk. In the United States, the legal limit is four times that amount. In Norway, a first offense can result in jail time and a one-year suspension of your driver's license. A second offense can land you in jail for a year, and you will lose your license forever. As a result, Norwegians don't take chances. Never in my life have I seen a Norwegian of any age have even a single drink and then get behind the wheel.

Norwegians in their late teens can legally drink alcohol in the presence of their parents, or licensed bartenders. They learn to handle their alcohol in safe situations before they are set free to engage in the inebriated rites of passage you are about to read about. In America, on the other hand, first journeys into alcohol tend to occur in hiding, with no supervision from experienced, more mature adults. This tends to result in vomit, which is really gross.

So there you have it. Now, grab yourself a beer or a glass of apple juice and enjoy these next two chapters. Or don't. You've been warned of the contents.

Oh, wait! Just one more thing. I would like to notify my parents that nothing in these next two chapters actually happened. It's all a bunch of embellished lies. I was a reclusive, nerdy kid who stayed home on Friday nights perfecting his Morse code speed, remember?

THE SNOW MUST GO ON

TRYSIL, NORWAY

5

Tor-Erik was trying to be helpful. I had asked all of my friends to please tell me when I said something wrong in Norwegian, but right now, I wasn't in the mood.

"Dave," he said as I asked the gas station attendant for a Snickers bar. "It's not Snickers. It's *Sneekersh.*"

"No it's not," I said.

"Yes it is."

"It's from America, Tor. You can correct my Norwegian but not my English."

I was in a cranky mood. We were supposed to be at the cabin by 4 p.m., but it was past seven now, with another hour to drive. A light snow was falling and the bright green Lada had conked out halfway to Trysil. We had just spent the last several hours hiking to the nearest gas station, having the car towed, and waiting for it to be fixed. I was starving.

The car must have broken down because we stressed its little engine. Ladas were not meant to carry five people, plus bags, skis, food, and approximately 2.7 tons of assorted alcoholic beverages. But we *needed* all of these supplies. We were on a mission to go commune with nature. For the next couple of days, I was going to experience my very first *hyttetur.*

Literally translated, *hyttetur* means "cabin trip." It's a favorite Norwegian pastime. Getting out and appreciating the land is as Norwegian as working overtime is American. It doesn't matter what the season is. Norwegians will go out and enjoy nature in any weather. It doesn't matter that their fingers have turned black from frostbite and their runny noses have formed two perfect, miniature icicles. Norwegians love the great outdoors. They're obsessed with the nature that surrounds them – the fjords, the mountains, the minus-20-degree temperatures.

I tell people about this in America, and I am often asked, "Dave, is that minus-20 Celsius or minus-20 Fahrenheit?" The answer to that question is: Who cares? Minus-20 degrees is just fucking cold. In America, we close schools when it's minus-20 degrees. In Norway, they put on skis and write songs about it.

Singing is a favorite Norwegian pastime. I've been at parties where people pass around song sheets. It's very Lawrence Welkish if you ask me, but the Norwegians I knew, even beer-guzzling teenagers, seemed seriously into composing original creations to impress their friends. They'd pass out photocopied lyrics at parties and expect everyone to sing their new, bastardized Norwegian words to, perhaps, "Oh When the Saints Go Marching In." Some songs were humorous "getting to know you" anthems about the other guests at the party. Others were words a guest had composed about the host. Once the original creations were exhausted, they would draw upon old folk melodies that pontificated upon the "It's a beautiful day in the forest" theme.

It's a beautiful day in the forest, tra la la la la,
And here we all are, tra la la la la,
And the sun is shining,
And the birds are chirping,
And the trolls are burping,
Tra la la la la.

It was a part of their culture I had to struggle to appreciate.

Right now though, nobody was singing. We were trying to go have an inspiring nature experience amid the snow and pine cones and several cases of alcohol, but the lawnmower engine that powered our Soviet-built Lada had conked out under the weight of too much vodka.

Finally, just as I was finishing my Sneekersh bar, the mechanic came out and told us he had finished duct taping the motor, and we could resume our excursion as soon as we paid him basically all the money in our wallets. We pooled our funds and squeezed back into the vehicle.

The cabin we were going to belonged to Ronny's parents. They weren't with us. They trusted us to behave unsupervised. This is another common Norwegian occurrence, and one I appreciated far more than the singing. Norwegian parents give their teens more freedom than American parents do, and in Norway, it works. Sure, on the trip we were now attempting, our idea of communing with nature involved staying drunk for 72 solid hours, but we would do so while hiking in the woods, or listening to the birds, or singing wholesome songs around the fireplace about the crunchy snow outside, tra la la. In America, teenagers were sitting in their bedrooms playing video games. And their American parents were *thinking* their kids were sober.

As we got back on the highway, we gained in elevation. Flurries turned to real snowflakes. An hour later, we came to what I worried might be our cabin; it looked rather ramshackle. But this was not our home for the weekend. It was a storage shed. Inside was a snowmobile we would use to go the last three miles to the cabin. Nobody had prepared me for a snowmobile ride, but beyond this point, the road was closed, buried under two feet of snow. This was the end of the line for the Lada.

It was 8:30 now. At least we were nearly there. I breathed a sigh of relief. As I was exhaling, Ronny shouted an all-too-familiar

Norwegian obscenity. My language skills were now good enough to understand such words.

"What's wrong?" his girlfriend, Kiki, asked.

"The shed's locked, and I don't have a key."

Was he kidding? After all that? A harrowing drive into the mountains, a long hike along the highway, a delay of several hours at a slimy gas station, the nervous pooling of our money to pay for the repairs, and a hard-fought struggle to keep our spirits high by reminding each other that soon we would be inebriated – after all that – there was no key to get into the shed that housed the snowmobile that would take us to our happy mountain home, tra la la?

"A neighbor was supposed to unlock it," Ronny said. "My parents called and told him we were coming. I'll have to go find him."

We stood and shivered. Ronny went in search of the neighbor.

"Shit, man," Tor-Erik said in English. I was developing a new appreciation for Tor's grasp of American slang.

Twenty minutes later, Ronny returned with a key to the shed. I stood outside and watched as the snowmobile was shoved into the cold.

Marius helped Ronny attach a sled to the back of the snow-mobile. It was long and thin, made of aluminum. Once it was connected, we loaded our supplies. Ronny took the driver's seat with Marius hanging on behind him. Tor-Erik, Kiki, and I found precarious spots on the sled…and we were off! We were zooming through the snowy wilderness at 30 miles per hour!

At 30 miles per hour, minus-20 degrees feels more like minus-200.

(Fahrenheit.) But I didn't care. We were almost at our shelter for the night. The wind invigorated me now as it penetrated my scalp and froze my eyeballs.

"Woooo!!" I shrieked, the way all teenage boys shriek when pretending to be happy that they are possibly about to die. "Wooooo! WOO HOOOOO!!!!...Oh shit!...*Brrlghf!*"

Then, everything went dark.

I couldn't tell for sure, but as I lay there in the pitch black cold – my mouth, ears, and nostrils all clogged with snow – I was thinking I might possibly be dead. I wiggled my toes to check. They were working. I plunged my hands down beneath me and somehow managed to wrestle my head up from the white, fluffy powder.

Marius and Ronny were still on the snowmobile, stopped on the trail about 30 feet ahead. Tor-Erik and Kiki were both sprawled out on the ground on the other side of the sleigh from me. Our gear was strewn in a path behind us, and the sled was on its side.

Ronny and Marius started running toward us.

"Are you okay?" Ronny shouted.

I looked to see if Kiki and Tor were alive. They were.

"Wooooo!!" I shouted.

We reloaded the sled and agreed our accident was cool. Ronny started driving again, more cautiously this time. A few minutes later, we reached our *hytte*.

It was a decent sized shack with two bedrooms, a living room, a kitchen, and an outhouse. Inside, the temperature was a balmy minus-10. I wasn't in the mood for manual labor, but there was work to be done. We had to open up the main water line into the cabin, carry in enough wood to feed the four wood-burning ovens through the night, and locate the key to the outhouse. The first task was easy. For the second, we formed a train, passing in logs and stoking the fireplaces.

Once the fires were going, the cabin warmed quickly. Now all we needed before we could relax was the key to the outhouse. Ronny looked under the kitchen sink. It wasn't there. He looked in a cupboard. It wasn't there either. He tried another cupboard. No key.

Finally, Ronny shrugged and looked apologetically at Kiki. "Sorry," he said. "We'll have to find a tree until morning."

Plumbing needs resolved temporarily, it was *finally* time to open our hard-earned beverages.

We each fell onto a random spot on the couch, cracked open bottles of Ringnes beer, and toasted. Marius cranked up some music by a Norwegian rock band. The fire crackled. We slurped, and smiled, and talked, the way people often talk to justify their alcohol intake, about how we *deserved* this moment. We had *earned* it. The beer was sweet, well chilled from several hours in the Lada trunk, and after our struggle to reach the cabin, we had finally arrived.

A couple of beers later, I could feel the tension seeping out of my muscles. I was filled with an incredible sense of calm. After all the stress of getting here, allowing myself to relax felt blissfully peaceful. So peaceful, I could almost hear it – a hissing noise, a release valve expelling all the day's stress.

When the song that was playing stopped, we looked around at each other. They were hearing it too – the peaceful hissing noise. One by one, the relaxed smiles on our faces began to shrivel.

"What's that?" Ronny asked to nobody in particular as he started toward the kitchen.

The peaceful hissing noise was not the sound of tension seeping from our bodies. It was the sound of water gushing from a broken pipe. The kitchen's wood floor had become a small pond, and the water was rising. It was spilling from a cabinet underneath the sink.

Ronny ordered us off the couch to help mop. I wanted to leave it until morning. It wasn't like we were going to drown. Once the water rose high enough, it would just make its way through the cabin walls or underneath the door, but Ronny explained that going back to our beer wasn't an option.

"It'll freeze to the floor if we leave it," he said.

"So?" I asked. "We can go ice skating."

But I was outvoted. We had to stop slurping and mop. We wrangled the water into buckets and then poured it into the kitchen sink.

Once the floor was dry and the main water valve disabled, we resumed our original course of events. Fires were raging in several wood-burning stoves, and the once-frigid cabin was toasty now.

To my relief, nobody had brought song sheets about the crispy snow outside. Our music was alternative rock, cranked full throttle on a boom box with a double portion of bass. Every so often, some-one would jump in and harmonize, in a Norwegian accent, coming as close to the real lyrics as they could. At some point, we must have decided to snooze for a few hours. I don't remember when, but I was the first person up the next morning.

My head felt foggy when I awoke. I was hungry, but I re-stoked the fires before scrounging in the fridge for food. Marius and Ronny emerged a little while later. They wanted coffee. Deprived of run-ning water, we retrieved snow from outside and brought it to a boil in the kitchen.

Sufficiently caffeinated, we bundled up in our winter clothes and poked our heads outside. It had been dark the night before when we arrived. Now in daylight, we could survey the land around us.

The sun shone brightly, raising the temperature to near zero degrees. (Kelvin.) The mountain air was still. It felt crisp against my lungs. We were surrounded by a dense forest of ancient fir trees. A blanket of snow muffled all sound, and a stillness, a pro-found sense of serenity, floated over the land.

We were alone, engulfed in nature. No one could disturb us here. This, I thought, was true freedom – standing here alone, engulfed by miles of pristine nature in every direction.

"Wait," Ronny said, "something's not right."

"I know," Marius said.

"What's wrong?" I asked.

"Hang on a second," Marius said as he retreated inside the cabin. "I'll fix it."

Seconds later, the boom box was outside, and Frank Zappa was screaming his rock 'n' roll vulgarities deep into the Norwegian woods. Bottles of Coke and Absolut Vodka were brought outside to further enhance our wilderness experience.*

*Oh, come on. You didn't think five teenagers with enough booze to stock a duty-free shop were going to go on a nature walk, did you?

Kiki and Tor-Erik awoke and joined us. We trampled down a swatch of snow in the yard and set up lawn chairs. We retrieved blankets from inside to keep warm. The sun burned its way down through the frigid air and warmed our faces while the snow kept our drinks chilled. We sat. We sipped. We sipped some more. We devised a system to ensure optimal slothishness. Whenever someone had to get up to take care of bladder-related needs, that person would also serve as bartender, so those whose glasses were near empty could remain seated.

Oh, but it wasn't all just sitting around and drinking. We got our share of physical activity in too. We devised a game that vaguely resembled American football, only there was no ball, and no goalpost, and come to think of it, we weren't really keeping score. The object was simply to tackle whomever was closest to you and smoosh their face into the snow. Then, you'd call time out before they could seek revenge, and everyone would have a drink.

On our last full day in Trysil, we decided we should send someone into town to get a replacement pipe for the sink. Ronny's parents had been kind enough to let us use their cabin. We wanted to leave it in good condition.**

**Oh, and also, we were almost out of beer. We needed to restock.

Marius and Ronny fired up the snowmobile and set off toward town. "We'll be back in an hour," Ronny shouted over the engine's rumble.

An hour passed. Then another... and a couple more. By early afternoon, the sun was sagging on the horizon.

We began to get concerned. What if they were lost? Or injured?

What if they'd rolled the snowmobile again and were unable to get their heads out of the snow? Which would kill them: frostbite or suffocation? It was too horrible to think about.

Kiki looked at me, pale with worry. "Do you think we should go look for them?"

"I guess we could," I said. "It's starting to get dark. Do you think we'd be safe?"

The snow was deep. The landscape looked identical in every direction – white and unchanging, a trillion trees fading into dusk. It would be easy to get lost. Searching for Ronny and Marius seemed dangerous. But if they were in trouble, darkness would soon swallow them.

I was afraid to leave the warmth of the cabin, but I was maturing, understanding that sometimes in life, you have to take risks. Certain things take priority over your own personal safety. If our friends were in trouble, we needed to find them. Fast. We all knew that if we didn't, in a matter of hours, we'd be completely out of beer.

"We must go look for them," I said.

"Dave and I can go," Tor-Erik told Kiki. "You stay here and keep the fires going."

Tor and I began putting on all the clothes we had. Once it got dark, it would be screaming cold. Just as I was slipping into my snow pants, the door swung open. Marius and Ronny were back, out of breath, lugging plumbing supplies, bread, and a fresh case of Ringnes. They looked exhausted – as if they'd been wrestling polar bears.*

"Where the hell have you been?" Kiki asked. "We were really worried."

"The snowmobile broke down," Marius said. "We had to hike back to the cabin."

"When will it be fixed?" I asked.

"In a couple of weeks."

"A couple of *weeks?* How are we supposed to get out of here?"

* Dear Norwegians,
Yes, I _know_ there are no polar bears on your country's mainland. Kindly resist the urge to send hate mail demanding that I correct the preceding analogy. Or if you must send hate mail, please enclose beer.
Love,
Dave

85

"We'll have to walk."

Was he crazy? Walk? Three miles through two feet of snow? No way. That's what people in my grandparents' generation did. I'll spare you the "uphill both ways" part.

Marius tried to calm me. "It's not that bad, Dave. We just hiked in from town. Most of the way, the snow was packed hard. We could walk on top of the snowmobile tracks."

As darkness fell, we decided we should rest up for the long trek the next morning. Even on packed snow, the walk would be tough with so much to carry – and nobody knew for sure if the snow pack would be thick enough to support our weight. If we couldn't walk on top of the snow, we'd be waist deep for three miles. So we agreed we should save our strength and make it an easy night. We spent the evening drinking apple juice, and singing songs about squirrels. We were in bed by 10:30.

Just kidding.

But seriously, to elaborate on our real activities would be redundant. Suffice it to say that the next morning, in spite of the arduous trudge ahead, we did the environmentally responsible thing, and loaded our empties onto the sleigh for recycling.

We each put on a backpack, and grabbed whatever else we could carry. Everything else went on the sleigh. Marius donned cross-country skis and lashed the sleigh's tow rope around his waist. We tied extra ropes to the back of the sleigh to help pull from behind.

Marius had been right. The snow was packed solid from our previous one-and-a-half snowmobile trips, and walking on top of the tracks was easy. We paused along the way for a picnic of salami and chocolate. Eventually, we reached the car and transferred everything inside. The Lada, considerably lighter now that our bottles were empty, coasted happily down the mountain, back to Drøbak.

I had just survived my first *hyttetur* – and in winter, no less. I was becoming a real Norwegian. I was even getting the language. But there was one rite of passage I had yet to experience. I had already graduated high school in the United States. As I was about to discover, however, finishing high school, Norwegian-style, would require a stamina they just don't teach in America.

MESSAGE IN A BOTTLE

SKI, NORWAY

The room was spinning and my vision was going dark. I heard a voice.

"Dave, do you have any more beer in your pocket?"

The voice sounded very far away.

"No," I sputtered. "I don't want beer right now. Please."

"No, Dave. This bottle just fell out of your pocket and broke. We need to be sure you don't have any more."

I rolled over on the naugahyde couch and looked down at a fizzy pile of broken glass. "Oh. Sorry."

"Just relax, Dave. Everything's going to be okay."

I hoped so. It was 5:30 in the morning. I hoped the high school principal wouldn't be angry that I had just smashed a beer bottle on his office floor.

Norwegians do high school graduation differently from Americans. They call it *russetid* – "time of the *russ*." *Russ* (rhymes with "moose") is a uniquely Norwegian word that basically translates to "teenagers on a not-entirely-prudent, yet socially accepted, partying binge."

The way it worked was you'd get together with a bunch of

friends and buy a van, known as a *russebil* or "*russ* car." You'd paint it red or blue, depending on what you had been studying in high school. There was a rivalry between the red *russ* and the blue *russ*. You would sell ad space to local businesses to help pay for the van, and paint their slogans on the side. Everybody would wear a *russedress* – red or blue coveralls – and a tasseled hat that looked ever-so-slightly less goofy than the mortar boards American grads wear on their heads. Each van would have a designated driver – someone from their class who didn't drink, or someone a year younger who wasn't graduating – and spend 17 sleep-deprived evenings cruising from party to party, celebrating the fact that high school was almost finished. Yes, almost. This all went down during the last two weeks of classes. Final exams began two days after *russetid* was finished.

For each 24-hour period you went without sleep, you earned the right to tie a knot in your tassel. If you stayed awake for 48 hours, you got a double knot. Drink a case of beer in 24 hours and you could tie a bottle cap in it. There were other tassel adornments for activities such as kissing a policeman, getting arrested, sleeping with a member of the *russ* organizing committee, or spending the night on a teacher's front lawn.

For me, *russetid* began as innocently as it could have begun for anyone. The first thing I had to do was learn to sew.

My bright red *russedress* arrived undecorated. It was tradition, Marius explained, to cut letters out of felt and sew your name on the leg, and your school's name on the back. For good measure, I sewed the word "*UTLENDING*" on the other leg – "FOREIGNER." Over the course of the year, I had adopted the self-ridiculing nickname. I wore it now as a badge of honor.

On the first night of our festivities, Knut pulled up in front of the house in our bright red van. Frank Zappa was screaming from the stereo system. The stereo cost more than the van itself. A *russebil* could be bought for cheap from the previous year's graduating class. If you wanted to make an impression, you didn't do it with an expensive vehicle. You did it with a deafening stereo.

The interior of the van was...let's call it "minimalist." There were two seats – one for the driver, and one for a passenger beside the driver. The back seats were removed, and the floor and walls were lined with beige shag carpeting. My fellow vanmates were an eclectic group. There were seven of us in all.

Knut was soft-spoken, not the sort you'd expect to party all night. He never touched alcohol, and we appreciated him for that. He was our default designated driver, always happy to take the wheel at 4 a.m. and transport us to our next gathering. Anders and Lars-Kåre were intelligent guys with a mischievous streak. Anders, like me, had an appreciation for alternative rock. We would band together at times to overrule Terje, whose tastes were more in the genre of the heaviest of metal. Ronny and Marius rounded out our crew.

There were parties. Don't ask me how many. It was hard to tell where one party ended and the next began. There were official gatherings – at bars or lakeside beaches. These were multi-school events with up to a thousand screaming teenagers. There were smaller affairs at people's houses. There were *vorspiel* and *nachspiel* – words the Norwegians borrow from German meaning "parties before the party" and "parties after the party." About a week into the whole mess, there was an impromptu overnight bonfire in the school parking lot.

The bonfire happened on a Thursday. There had been a party at a dance club in Moss, a town 20 miles south of Drøbak. Students from three schools were there. It lasted until 2 a.m., at which point someone realized we didn't have to be in class for another six hours. What were we supposed to do until then? So we spread the word. We arranged a *russebil* convoy back to Ski, the town where our school was.

Ski was a nondescript town in a not-so-picturesque setting away from the fjord, but our school parking lot was surrounded by a woodsy area. There was plenty of firewood. The next thing I knew, it was 3 a.m. The sun was rising and we were huddled around a giant fire.

By 4:30, we had a crisis. There was no more beer. Asking other people for beer had not occurred to me, but three girls from another *russebil* had no shame.

"Hey Dave," Linda said with a seductive smile, "it's really been wonderful getting to know you this year."

"Sorry Linda," I said. "I'm out of beer like everybody else."

Her seductive smile faded. "Oh. Well come with us then. We're on a mission."

Linda, Pam, and Line were three girls from my class. "We met these guys from Nesodden. They were all passed out earlier and they had beer left then."

Linda and I peered in the window of their van while Pam and Line waited a safe distance away. Inside the van were three guys – snoring, drooling, with heads hanging to the side in neck-cramp-inducing poses.

"*Shhh,*" Linda said, holding her index finger over her mouth. "They're already going to have nasty hangovers. They'll thank us for this later."

Careful not to disturb the occupants, Linda pried open the van door with the quiet finesse of a soldier disarming a bomb. The boys didn't budge. There was a case of beer bottles on the van floor. Two bottles were still full.

"Hide these in your *russedress,*" Linda said. "Don't tell Line and Pam."

Every *russedress* came with a special pocket on the side of the right leg, designed for holding a beer bottle. I stashed one bottle there, the other in a regular pocket.

"What's up?" Pam asked as we emerged around the corner.

"They were out of beer," Linda lied. "Look, Dave and I are going to take a walk."

"Huh?"

"Ummm, yeah. He's going back to America soon and I have to tell him I've been secretly in love with him all year."

"With Dave?"

"Yeah." Linda turned to me and put her arm around me. "Come on, Dave."

We wandered off into the surrounding woods.

"Where's the beer?" she asked.

I retrieved the two bottles from my pockets.

Linda's love for me would only last as long as I possessed both bottles, but that was okay. She was sharing something more meaningful than love. She was sharing the last two clandestine beers, in a sea of drunken teenagers, the still-conscious of whom were desperately searching for more to drink.

The sun rose higher on the horizon. The next thing I knew, it was time for class.

"Please take out a pen and some paper," said our religion teacher, Herr Schou. "It's time for a pop quiz."

A look of panic washed over a few faces. Other students just shrugged. Everybody flunked.

Throughout the day, the graduating class staggered around the school in a glassy-eyed stupor. People fell asleep in class, or on the benches where we gathered between classes. By late morning, the teachers had figured out about our all-night bender. An emergency assembly was called.

"I have never seen a class of *russ* behave so irresponsibly!" a teacher bellowed from behind a podium.

We all shifted in our seats, doing all we could to stifle our giggles.

"If this happens again," the teacher continued, "all other *russ* celebrations will be canceled."

With that threat, a more serious quiet settled in the room.

"Staying out all night, getting wasted, lighting a fire in the school parking lot, and inviting *russ* from two other schools to come make a mess at our school is not appropriate!"

I could see his point.

"That is *not* something you do on May 6th!"

Definitely not.

"It is what you do on May 14th."

Huh?! My Norwegian was good by this point, but surely I had misunderstood that last part.

"We understand this is an important time in your lives," the teacher continued, "but you are still in school, and you cannot have bonfires in the parking lot until the last day of classes is fin-ished. Until then, you will have to have your parties elsewhere."

This was definitely not American-style high school graduation. We weren't in trouble for getting drunk and lighting fires at school. We were in trouble for doing so prematurely.

So we obeyed the administration's rules. Our parties contin-ued away from school property. Eight days, and roughly 17 hours of sleep later, May 14 arrived. It was a Friday – the last day of classes and the start of a three-day weekend. On May 17, Norway would commemorate the drafting of its constitution with parades, speeches, and the mother of all *russ* parties.

I had acquired two knots in my tassel over the last two weeks for two separate 24-hour periods without sleep. I was determined to have knot number four by Monday morning. On the last day of classes, we charged out of school, dove into our *russebil*, and took off for a pre-party, followed by a party at a local discothèque, fol-lowed by another bonfire. There was no doubt this time around. Tonight, it was okay to trash the parking lot.

Sleep deprivation had taken hold in epidemic proportions. For the last two weeks, we had gone to class in the day, and parties most nights. I had slowed down my beer intake. The weekend was just starting. I needed to pace myself if I was going to get my other two knots.

Around 2 a.m., Marius found me in the school parking lot. "Dave," he said, "we're going to Drøbak to shower. We'll be back in a couple of hours."

"I want to come," I said. With a weekend of spontaneity ahead, I sensed this might be one of my only opportunities for hygiene.

"Okay," Marius said. "I need to find Thomas, and then I'll come get you."

Thomas, my older host brother, was home from the military and had stowed away in our *russebil*.

An hour later, I looked around for Marius. I spotted Lars-Kåre.

"Hey Lars!" I shouted across the parking lot. "Have you seen Marius?"

"He and Thomas went to Drøbak. They'll be back in a couple of hours."

Unable to find me among the sea of people all dressed in the same red coveralls, they had gone without me.

"Damn it!" I grumbled. "Did they try to find me or did they just take off? I told them I wanted to go with them."

"Relax, Dave," my friend Børre said. "Here. Have a beer."

I sulked. I was exhausted, craving a shower, desperately wanting to connect with home if only for a few hours. I pictured them driving down the road – halfway home – without me. At that moment, I wanted nothing more than to be in the *russebil,* speeding my way toward a quick nap.

I inched closer to the bonfire. I talked with friends. I talked with strangers. Next thing I knew, it was 5 a.m. I was in a huddle with Børre's punk rock pals when Gaute came and tapped me on the shoulder.

"Gaute!" I shouted. *"Skål!"*

"Dave," he said, "I need you to come with me."

"Skål, Gaute!" I said again, raising my bottle.

"Dave, come inside the school with me. It's important."

"Inside the school? School's finished, Gaute! I'm not going in there!"

Gaute took a deep breath and lowered his voice. "There's been an accident. Marius and Thomas are in the hospital."

Gaute loved practical jokes, but this wasn't something he would joke about. My heart began pounding. This night had been the culmination of the most fun I had ever had. In an instant, the fun disintegrated.

"What happened?" I asked, switching to English.

"They were driving to Drøbak and they crashed your *russebil*. We're trying to contact the hospital to find out the details. We know they're both still alive."

Another student was in the office, talking on the phone. The news wasn't good. There had been five people in the van – Marius and Thomas; Marius's girlfriend, Anne; Terje; and Gunhild, a girl who had taken over as designated driver. They were all alive, but Thomas was unconscious. He had been thrown from the vehicle. A helicopter had airlifted him to the hospital.

As the news sank in, along with the realization that I had planned to go with them, that I could have just been killed – *killed* – the world started swirling around me. My peripheral vision turned fuzzy and black. I lay down on the couch. My breathing turned to panicked panting.

"I need a bag," I said, sticking with English. I was too upset to speak Norwegian. Several other students gathered around, trying to comfort me.

"Are you going to be sick?" a voice asked. I couldn't tell who it was. Everything was blurring. My fingers were going numb.

"No, I feel like I'm going to faint. I'm hyperventilating."

A trash can was thrust under my nose. As good as everyone's English was, "to hyperventilate" was not a verb they had learned in English class.

"No." I pushed the trash can away. "I'm hyperventilating. I'm breathing too fast. I need a bag."

"It's okay," a voice echoed from afar. "If you're going to be sick, you can use this."

I lay down and moaned, trying to breathe normally.

"Dave," I heard another voice say. "Do you have any more beer in your pocket?"

"No. I don't want beer right now. Please."

"Dave, is there any more beer in your *russedress?*"

I looked up. It was a friend of Marius.

"How can you ask me for beer at a time like this?"

"No, Dave, a beer fell out of your pocket."

The bottle had shattered all over the principal's office.

Marius and Terje were released from the hospital later that day – Terje with a broken arm, Marius with some nasty scrapes and bruises. Thomas and Anne were both in the hospital for a couple of weeks with back injuries. Thomas also had a concussion, but given the circumstances, they were all lucky to be alive. Gunhild, who had been driving, walked away relatively unscathed, feeling far more guilt than she deserved.

Gunhild never drank alcohol. The police determined there'd been nothing wrong with her driving. The brakes had failed, sending the van careening down a hill and crashing into a small cement barrier at a traffic circle.

After the accident, local newspapers raised valid questions. Yes, having a designated driver was imperative, but what about overall *russebil* safety? The vans were sold at bargain prices from one graduating class to the next, handed down like outgrown sweaters. Sweaters wear out over time, and so do brakes.

Norway's State Highway Authority has taken steps over the years to address the problem. Among other things, they now offer free safety checks during *russetid* to ensure the vehicles are safe.

The event rattled me emotionally. Everybody survived the crash with injuries which, given the circumstances, were remarkably minor. Had I been in the car, would I have been so lucky? I'll never know.

Graduation ceremonies were three weeks later. I gave a speech in Norwegian to 200 students and their parents. My hands trembled, but I did not hyperventilate. I had just survived the second year of my life as an expat.

The principal spotted me after the ceremony. This was it. The confrontation. He was a formal, serious man. I grappled for the right words...as if there were right words. Is there an appropriate way to apologize to your high school principal for smashing a beer bottle in his office?

I was probably in trouble, and not the good kind of trouble. Most people who got in trouble during *russetid* got to tie something in their tassel, but I would receive no such badge of honor for this offense. This was a new one. And the sad thing was I had paced my drinking carefully that night. I had not been guzzling to excess. It was the shock of the accident that had triggered my tailspin.

"Dave," the principal said as he shook my hand, "I hope you have enjoyed your year here. We have enjoyed having you."

That was all. Either he hadn't heard about the bottle incident, or he had decided to ignore it.

The principal's words, his sternness, his formal nod that came with his handshake, warranted a dignified response. But the only Norwegian I could muster from my teenage mouth was, "Thanks. It's been a cool year."

That's what happens when you learn a language from slang-obsessed teenagers. But the principal chuckled at my linguistic gaffe.

"Det har vært kult å treffe deg, Dave," he said. "It's been cool meeting you."

PART III

AN ADULT-IN-TRAINING

1989

F reshman year at the University of Wisconsin-Madison was a blast. I liked my classes. I wrote for the campus newspaper. I had a healthy, Morse code–free social life.

Sophomore year didn't go so smoothly.

For starters, there was Jennifer. I had sort of been dating Jenn freshman year. I say "sort of" because I'm not sure she considered us a couple. She called me from Alaska during the summer between freshman and sophomore years with the happy news that her Alaskan boyfriend was moving to Wisconsin.

Then came the death threats. They were from a campus fraternity. ZBT pledges had painted their faces black and auctioned themselves off as slaves on the town square. In my newspaper column, I wrote that such racism shouldn't be tolerated. They responded with middle-of-the-night phone calls to inform me that auctioning off black-faced white boys as slaves was *not* racist. It wasn't, it wasn't, it *wasn't!* And to prove that they really were decent, upstanding citizens, they were coming to kill me.

Dorm life wasn't going well either. The dorms had been fun freshman year, but by sophomore year, I was outgrowing them. I tried moving, thinking maybe the problem was the other people on my floor, but my new dorm housed every cocaine addict in Madison. Every day from noon to 4 a.m., my next-door neighbor would blast bad 1980s hair bands on his 16-quadzillion-watt stereo. "All we need is just a little patience," crooned Guns and Roses lead singer Axl Rose.

The last straw was the chicken pox. I'd avoided the disease as a kid, but now it caught up to me. "We have to quarantine you to your floor," a nurse told me when I called the Student Health Service. "If you come in contact with someone who has AIDS or is receiving certain cancer treatments, you could kill them."

I didn't want to kill anybody, other than maybe my next door neighbor and a few select frat boys, but my dorm had no cooking facilities. How would I eat if I couldn't leave the floor?

"Your friends on your floor can bring you food," the nurse said.

I was too embarrassed to tell her I had no friends on my floor.

Heartbreak, death threats, chicken pox, Axl Rose...any one of those was enough to trigger a breakdown. With all four in rapid succession, depression set in. I came to an important conclusion. If I did not die of starvation during my week in quarantine,* I needed to make some changes. The prudent solution to my problems – obviously – was to run away to Iceland.

*which I did not, thanks to friends who lived elsewhere on campus

I had almost chosen Iceland instead of Norway as the place to spend my exchange student year. My exchange program's area representative had talked me out of it. The country fascinated me, however, I think because it was the kind of place normal Americans did not go. Some kids rebelled by doing drugs. I rebelled by doing Iceland.

My escape plan expanded. If I was going to Iceland, I might as well see Turkey. And points in between. And hell, I should write a book. Why not? I had just scored an A in Journalism 101.

Professor Cook eyed me skeptically when I told him of that plan.

"You might want to start with some shorter magazine articles," he suggested. He didn't have the heart to tell me what I think he knew – that I was insane. But he agreed to be my advisor for an independent study project when I returned home.

I cut back on my studies to work. I saved enough cash for a

plane ticket, a Eurail pass, and 26 dollars a day for food and lodging. *Let's Go: Europe,* the self-proclaimed "Bible of the budget traveler," recommended a higher daily minimum, but it was 26 bucks a day or no trip. Next stop: Reykjavík.

The airplane banked left, and I caught my first glimpse of the rocky island nation. We'd be landing in just a few minutes. But something wasn't right. For starters, there were no puffins.

Every Icelandic tour brochure showed puffins. They were chubby, whimsical creatures – crosses between squat penguins and VW Bugs. They were supposed to be waiting with smiles on their beaks, waving welcome signs and offering me a toast with the controversial substance Icelanders had just legalized after a 74-year ban: beer.

But there were no puffins. There was no beer. There wasn't even a Reykjavík.

My guidebook told me Reykjavík's airport was a mile from downtown. You could get to the city center via bus or taxi, but to me, landing in a foreign city and simply hiking along the highway into town sounded like the rugged Indiana Jones way to begin my adventure. It wasn't until we started circling to land that I realized Reykjavík, a small capital, but an existent one nonetheless, was missing.

The problem was we weren't landing in Reykjavík. International flights touched down at a military airport an hour away. I'd have to catch a shuttle bus to the Reykjavík airport before I could begin my trek to the city center. Our wheels screeched a couple of times on the runway, and we rolled to the gate.

Iceland was waking up to a new day, but in the United States, it was the middle of the night. The world felt wobbly and surreal. The ground seemed to swell up and down in soft waves of sleep deprivation. As the bus zoomed toward Reykjavík, I tried to snooze, propping my head against the window, but the road was full of potholes. My head banged against the glass, and I wondered which would crack first – the window or my skull.

"This is good," I told myself. "It's keeping me awake."

A dizzying hour later, we rolled into Reykjavík's airport. A cold wind growled as I stepped off the bus. I was prepared for the climate – as long as I stayed inside. Outside was another matter. I had followed the official Rick Steves Packing List.

I had met Rick Steves a few months earlier when he had come to Madison to give a talk on budget travel. He had not yet attained the travel guru status he now enjoys. His "Pack Light" travel sermons were good advice for people starting their European journeys in Europe. It hadn't occurred to me as I packed that Iceland was an unsheltered rock in the middle of the North Atlantic. Gale force winds were blasting down from the North Pole. I retrieved a flimsy jacket from my backpack and began my trek along the highway.

Iceland only has one highway. It's called *Hringbraut* – the Ring Road – because it rings the periphery of the country. It paves a path over steaming, earthquake-shredded lava fields that are coated with a thin, sallow moss.

Stubborn grasses grew by the roadside, clinging to the earth in spite of the winds. I tried to be strong, like the grass. But the grass was used to this sort of abuse. I wasn't. I had a thin cotton sweater and a joke of a jacket. I stopped every few steps to wipe my nose and brush wind-bullied tears from my eyes. I was shivering. I was exhausted. I was in Iceland.

What the hell was I doing in Iceland?

Couldn't I take a normal European vacation? Hundreds of other Americans were starting trips in warm, sunny places like the French Riviera or the Greek islands. That's probably where the puffins were too.

Twenty minutes later, I reached downtown. Modern billboards peddled Coca-Cola and newspapers in the medieval Icelandic script.

"Walk up Flugvallarbraut, turn left on Hringbraut, and turn right on Laufásvegur," my guidebook instructed. All I had to do was turn two corners, but I was too zonked to read signs with words like "Flugvallarbraut."

I shuffled past the American Embassy, past banks and bakeries, past business people scurrying to work. I circled a few city blocks in the general vicinity of the hostel. I wasn't finding it. Then, like magic, I turned a corner and spotted a sign a block away with the International Youth Hostel logo.

That's when it hit me: I had no clue what I was doing. I had 90 days ahead of me, a railpass, a map, a backpack full of clothes, notebooks, and camera gear, and not a single reservation or commitment. I had just crossed the line between fantasy and reality.

Three months later, I would return to Wisconsin with six notebooks full of stories. I'd spend the next two years crafting those journals into a book manuscript – 550 double-spaced pages, printed on a dot matrix printer that screamed as it printed like an irate chimpanzee. In the end, I would find myself faced with the sad reality that I had just broken a useless world record – the longest version in history of "What I Did On My Summer Vacation." It was a book that could never sell.

But the stories have remained, tucked away at the bottom of a drawer. So I've untucked a few of them, dusted them off, and done my best to weed out the self-absorbed drivel of a 20-year-old, replacing it with the self-absorbed drivel of a 39-year-old. Here are a few of those stories.

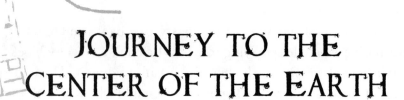

JOURNEY TO THE CENTER OF THE EARTH

HEIMAEY, ICELAND

The women behind the snack bar couldn't restock the little paper buckets fast enough.

The buckets were for puking in. As an alternative, a dozen or so school children were leaning over the side of the boat, crying, vomiting into the North Sea, and trying to dodge their regurgitated breakfasts, which the wind was flinging back at them.

I worried I'd be next.

The waves had been tossing our little ferry around for more than an hour. I had seasickness medicine, but I didn't want to take it unless absolutely necessary. It knocked me out. So instead, I tried to focus on the happy side of seasickness. The group of 50 kids – rambunctious and hyper when they boarded the ferry – was subdued now.

Their chaperones didn't seem affected by the waves. I supposed the adults had made the journey enough times to be immune. Or maybe they hoarded their seasickness tablets for themselves and had a good laugh at the retching 12-year-olds. Either way, I didn't envy them for having to mop up after the kids who couldn't make it to the front of the boat in time.

One by one, children were turning green and dashing outside, hands covering their mouths in a last, futile attempt to keep every-thing in. They were lined up – 10 or 12 of them – all heaving into the water. I watched from inside with morbid curiosity, until I was gripped by the fear that I had waited too long to take my own medicine. A mild nausea had simmered in the lower recesses of my belly for a while. Now it was really beginning to gurgle.

"*Talarðu ensku eða norska?*" I asked the woman behind the snack bar. Do you speak English or Norwegian? It was one of my two Icelandic phrases.

"*Nei,*" she smiled.

"*Vann?*" I asked, hoping the Norwegian word for water would be close enough. I just needed to wash down my pill.

"*Vatn?*" she asked.

"*Ja!*" I answered, hoping *vatn* and *vann* really were the same thing. The previous night in Reykjavík, I had woken up thirsty, wandered down to the youth hostel kitchen, and nearly taken a big swig of ammonia from a refilled juice bottle on a shelf marked, "communal food."

The woman smiled and pointed to the sink. "*Vatn?*" she asked again.

"*Ja!*" I said more insistently. "*Vatn! Vatn!*"

She turned on the tap. She let the water flow. She smiled some more.

I tried to smile back.

The water was running. The lady was smiling. My stomach was gurgling. I scrunched my face into my best "Please give me water *now* before I lose my breakfast all over your counter" look.

The nice lady smiled some more.

She was waiting for the water to cool down to a more palatable temperature, but I didn't need icy, refreshing goodness. I needed anything of the non-scalding variety that would help wash down my pill.

I should have learned more Icelandic. Just a few phrases. "It's nice to meet you. I am seasick. If you don't give me water, I am going to hurl." Instead, I stood there helpless, afraid to resort to travelers' sign language. Miming seasickness just might trigger the real thing.

Finally I got my water and downed my pill. I went back to my seat to stare out of a salty porthole at the churning sea and the puking children on deck.

I was traveling to Heimaey, an island off of Iceland's south coast. Heimaey had been the scene of an unexpected volcanic eruption in 1973. The island's 5,600 residents hadn't expected the eruption because the day before, there hadn't even been a volcano. That was life in Iceland. You never knew when or where the earth might split apart. On a cold January night, the ground just cracked open and began spewing lava.

Sixteen years later, most of the islanders had now returned to Heimaey. They were living peacefully in the shadow of the still-steaming monster. I couldn't understand why anybody would return to a place where the volcano that had devoured their homes could blow again at any moment. I was traveling to Heimaey to interview the people and write an article about them.

Chuming the Waters

#1 tourist pastime

I survived the three-hour maritime roller coaster. I wobbled off the boat in search of fresh air. As I stepped back onto land, I was greeted by more fresh air than I knew what to do with. Pounding winds were whipping up little black pebbles that attacked me like pissed-off mosquitoes. The pebbles pecked at any exposed flesh, leaving little red welts. The volcanic sand was everywhere, lingering since the 1973 eruption, swirling in the air until it spotted me. I swear the flying gravel had some sort of magical volcanic homing device. "Look," the leader of one clump of gravel would say to the other pebbles. "A tourist! Get him!" Then, hundreds of tiny black rocks would all fling themselves at me.

In the distance, I could see the volcano. It steamed with an ominous peacefulness. It looked like a giant ant hill – a black mound of hardened but not-completely-cooled lava. The centerpiece of the island, it sat there stoically amid the pounding wind-and-gravel storm, as if to say, "I am your planet. Don't fuck with me."

I set off in search of my "guesthouse."

I didn't know what to expect in terms of accommodations. The island's youth hostel was not yet open for tourist season. The receptionist at the Reykjavík hostel had booked me into the cheapest place available.

The guesthouse turned out to be luxurious by my budget-travel standards – my own room with clean sheets, and screaming young women down the hall.

I followed the noise and poked my head around the corner. Two women around my age looked up at me. I said hello.

Raina and Laila were from Denmark. They were working for a year at a Reykjavík nursing home. They had arrived on Heimaey two days earlier in search of volcanoes and booze. Their four friends were down the hall, sleeping off hangovers.

"I just got here," I said. "I don't really know what I'm doing. Is there any place where I can get some food?"

"This place is pretty cheap," Laila said, pointing out a spot on my map. "We ate there yesterday. We're going for dinner in a couple of hours when our friends wake up. You can come with us if you want."

I was hungry. I hadn't eaten since breakfast. But for six drunken women, I could wait.

Once the other four emerged from their cocoons, they took me to dinner. They were all around my age, all hyper, and apparently on a mission to avoid sobriety at all costs. "Have you tried the Icelandic beer yet?" one of them asked me.

I hadn't.

"You know, they just legalized it."

Just two months earlier, the Icelandic parliament had struck down a 74-year ban on beer. March 1, 1989, had been the biggest party the country had ever seen – so big that even veteran TV journalist Peter Jennings showed up, anchoring "World News Tonight" from a Reykjavík bar.

The odd thing was that prior to the lifting of the beer ban, Icelanders could drink as much wine and hard liquor as they wanted. The national firewater was a potent concoction called Black Death. But the only beer that was legal in Iceland was non-alcoholic. People found a way to deal with this annoyance. They spiked their alcohol-free beer with vodka.

There were historical reasons behind the beer ban. In 1915, Iceland's government had imposed all-out prohibition. This annoyed Spain, which had been exporting a lot of wine to Iceland. So Spain issued an ultimatum: Keep buying our wine or we stop buying your stockfish.

Stockfish was a dried, salted cod – a "fish jerky" of sorts. It didn't need refrigeration and was therefore a dietary staple in many European countries. It was one of Iceland's few resources to trade internationally. Out of economic necessity, Iceland's government buckled under Spain's demands. They legalized wine again so Spain would buy their fish.

A few years later, France pulled a similar stunt with cognac. Hard liquor in Iceland was once again made legal. But none of the beer-producing nations seemed interested in economic threats, so for decades, beer had remained illicit.

In recent years, beer had sparked time-consuming debates in Parliament. The Committee on Alcohol Awareness had led the anti-beer movement, fearful beer would spawn inebriated business lunches and encourage drunk driving. The legalization question came up for a Parliamentary vote several years in a row. Each time, the government voted to maintain the spike-your-non-alcoholic-beer-with-vodka status quo. Then, an Icelandic businessman successfully argued he had a constitutional right to drink beer.

The businessman flew in from London, brazenly flaunting a six-pack. When officials tried to confiscate it, he pointed out that Iceland's constitution said all citizens were equal. Icelanders who worked for international transportation companies – pilots and flight attendants, for example – were allowed to bring one six-pack into the country on each trip. If you didn't work in an approved industry, however, customs authorities would confiscate your brew, and probably go have a big party after work. This businessman argued that if some citizens could import beer, all citizens must be granted equal rights.

In the end, Icelanders have told me, Parliament legalized beer, not so much because of the constitutional issue, but because they were sick of arguing about it. What I've never been able to ascertain is, once they started brewing beer with alcohol, did they stop pouring vodka into it?

Egil's Brewery was now pumping out a new national beverage. It tasted like beginner's homebrew – not quite there yet, but a respectable attempt for a company that had only been brewing the real stuff for a couple of months. We moved from the restaurant to a local pub, where my new-found harem told me about the island.

"Have you been to the volcano yet?" asked Katrine, another one of the Danes. "You can go down inside the crater."

"You can go into the crater?"

"Yeah. We did it today."

I added a journey into the crater to my to-do list for the next day.

It was getting late. "I should go," I said. "I've got a lot of work tomorrow."

"But you're not working right now," Laila said. She bought me another beer, and then, another, with a side order of Black Death. At 1:30 a.m., the bartender kicked us out.

All was quiet when I fell out of bed in the morning. I could hear my housemates snoring down the hall. I needed to get moving. As I showered, gravel fell from my hair like black dandruff.

I had two tasks to accomplish today: Climb the volcano, and interview people.

I could see the volcano from the town center. An eerie steam wafted around it. Steep, crumbling slopes reached toward the sky, almost meeting at the crater. The winds had mellowed since the previous day, but they were still blowing. Ignoring the cold, and the wind, and the menacing gravel, I zipped my flimsy jacket and began hiking.

At the base of the volcano, the ground was solid, and walking was easy. Grass was attempting to grow. A dirt road was cut part way up. Eventually, I reached a line where solid earth ended. Above it, the hill became a giant pile of loose gravel. It was hard to walk on. I'd take a step forward and my feet would slither back several inches. Tiny stones spilled over into the edges of my shoes, and every 50 feet or so, I'd have to stop and empty them.

Above me, I spotted a ridge. When I reached the top, I looked out over a moonlike valley, carved out where the lava had bull-dozed its way through town. It was the same blacker-than-a-cat rock I had just been climbing on, but as I crossed to the other side of the ridge, the ground became solid, not gravelly. It was splotched with a spooky, pale yellow moss that clung to the sharp land where nothing else dared grow. Across the lava field, a valley led to the crater. A hundred feet beneath me were 400 houses the volcano had gobbled up.

There was nobody else up here. Just me and the volcano. Nobody within sight in any direction. The wind was pummeling my eardrums. Remnants of the previous night's Black Death were fogging my brain, but I didn't care. I also didn't care that I had no knowledge whatsoever of how to climb a volcano. I kept going.

The ground around me was still warm. In isolated spots, col-umns of steam wafted from the earth. I touched one of the spots. It burned my fingertips.

I continued toward the crater. The slope grew steeper until I was walking at an awkward angle. I dug the sides of my feet into the gravel, leaning into the face of the mountain, at times using my hands as well to scramble upward. I was getting close – maybe 30 feet from the top. That's when I looked down.

I shouldn't have looked down.

Was I insane?! I didn't know how to climb a volcano. Given the previous night's activities, it was a wonder I could climb stairs right now. I had no clue how I had just gotten up here. For the last hour, I had been climbing in a hungover stupor. And the sulfuric fumes were making me delirious. What was I thinking?

I looked up at the summit. It wasn't far, but getting there looked impossible. The gravel was too loose and the slope was too steep. Had Katrine really been into the crater or had she just had too many shots of Black Death?

I guessed the latter. I needed to find a way down. But how could I get down when I wasn't even sure how I had gotten up? If the gravel beneath me started to slide, I could sprain an ankle and not be able to walk. If I fell, the jagged rock would slice and dice me like a Ginsu knife. The roar of the wind would stifle my cries for help. It could be days before anybody found me. I started trembling. The volcano had not killed anybody during the 1973 eruption. I wondered if I'd be the first.

I felt trapped. I wanted a helicopter, or an escalator, or a Disneyland-style gondola. I realized I had two options: figure out a way down and risk the descent, or curl up in the fetal position and whimper. A voice of safety was pushing for the curl-and-whimper strategy, but I had a boat to catch at five. I started to navigate my descent.

"Quit whimpering," I scolded myself. "Do you want your eyes to be all puffy from crying when they discover your broken body at the bottom?"

I made it down, with only a few scrapes and scorched fingertips. Back on solid ground, I wandered through a residential area past stucco houses with corrugated metal roofs. Cracks in the houses were patched with cement, but never painted to match the old color. The cracks were like scars, souvenirs of the past, scruffy monuments to survival, and a constant reminder that ultimately, nature could kick our collective human butt.

Evidence of the eruption was everywhere. In the cemetery, the islanders had not been able to bulldoze the rock away. It would have damaged the tombstones. So people came instead with spades and whisk brooms, daintily removing the gravel, one small shovelful at a time.

Of the 5,600 residents who fled the volcano that fiery night in January, 1973, 5,000 had returned. Four-hundred houses were lost, forever entombed in a river of now-hardened lava. Hundreds more homes had been partially covered. Once the eruption stopped, the islanders returned to dig out.

At the harbor, I met Rafn. He was an electrician in one of the island's two fish meal factories. We started chatting. He recalled the night the volcano blew.

"I was sleeping," he said. "A friend of my brother knocked on the window and told me there was a volcano erupting. He had been at a birthday party and we thought he was drunk. He told us, 'Come see for yourself.' We looked out, and...*whooeee!!* We saw fire."

Rafn's brother owned a station wagon – the only car on the island, other than the one ambulance, that was big enough to transport hospital patients to the rescue boats. So the two had stayed through the night helping evacuate the hospital while most residents fled. Six months later, they were two of the first people to return.

"It was like a ghost town," Rafn said. "Everything was black."

I didn't get it. You're lying in a peaceful slumber when all of a sudden, your crazed neighbor is pounding on your bedroom window. Outside, the planet is on fire. There's no time to gather your belongings. Get to the harbor and cross the sea. Watch your village go up in flames as you retreat into the distance. It was a trauma few people could fathom, yet most of Heimaey's residents had gone back.

I wandered further, looking for others to interview. Every person I met had the same reaction.

"It was fantastic to look at," said a man named Ægir. "It was beautiful."

Ægir was 13 when the volcano erupted. His house had been buried to the roof in ash, but afterward, his family had cleared the ash away. He still lived in the same house. You could see the volcano from his front yard.

"Doesn't it make you nervous to come outside every day and see the volcano?" I asked.

"I hardly notice it."

Ægir's neighbor, Mary, was the only person I met who seemed perturbed by the volcano. Eight months pregnant at the time of the eruption, she and her four-year-old daughter had fled in a rescue boat.

"I thought those hours would be my last," she said, struggling with her English.

Finally! Finally someone was being honest!

"You were afraid!" I prompted.

"No," Mary said.

"But you just said you thought you were going to die."

"Yes! I was very seasick!"

That was the traumatic part? A volcano was swallowing her entire town...and her worst memory was that she felt *seasick?!* Hell, even a wimp like me had survived the boat ride. I couldn't take these people's stoicism anymore. I was trying to be polite. I was trying to coax their stories from them gently. But I wanted to scream. "There's a big honking volcano in your back yard! It's still warm! I burned my fingers on it two hours ago! It trashed your neighborhood! It could do it again! What the hell are you doing here?"

I refrained from using those exact words, however, and posed my question in a more refined way. Why, I asked Mary, did she return to Heimaey, to live right down the street from a volcano?

115

She looked annoyed with my question. "I was homesick. Besides, this is Iceland. A volcano can happen anywhere, anytime. It could happen tomorrow in Reykjavík."

In the late afternoon, I started toward the guesthouse to get my bag. The Seasick Express departed in an hour.

"Where have you been all day?" shouted Laila as I wandered up the hill. She and her posse were headed to the port to catch the same boat as me.

"I've just been wandering and talking to people," I said.

"Did you climb the volcano?" asked Katrine.

"Yeah. It was incredible."

"Did you go into the crater?"

"I tried. It was too steep."

"It wasn't so steep."

Clearly this girl was hallucinating.

"You did *not* go into the crater," I said. "It's impossible."

"We did!"

"How? It's dangerous up there!"

Katrine rolled her eyes.

"You seriously made it down?" I asked. "Inside the crater?" We had been communicating in a mixture of English, Norwegian, and Danish. Maybe we just weren't understanding each other.

"Dave," Laila said in English, "you can go into the crater. We all did it. Maybe you just went the wrong way."

The wrong way? Maybe if I approached from the other side I could make it. But my boat was leaving in 50 minutes.

"Is it really worth seeing?" I asked.

"Not if you have volcanoes in Wisconsin you can climb."

"Do you think I can make it in time and still catch the boat?"

"If you want, we'll carry your bag to the harbor so you don't have to go back and get it."

I pondered. Six people I barely knew were offering to relieve me of all my belongings as they boarded a boat I was possibly about to miss.

"What if I don't get to the boat in time?"

"We'll leave your backpack at the ticket desk."

Could I do it? Race to the volcano, climb to the top, get into the crater, back down, and then across to the port on the other side of the island in one hour? No way. But instead of listening to logic, I listened to a cute Danish woman. I gave Katrine my bag and took off running.

I did the math as I ran. My morning climb had taken 90 minutes, but I knew the way now. I knew how to negotiate the loose gravel and jagged rocks. I let the pebbles fill my shoes. There was no time to empty them.

I reached the mossy part on the ridge of hardened lava. I stood and rested for a second, scanning the landscape. I wasn't sure if I was seeing...I put on my glasses...yes, there were footprints – probably the Danes' from the day before. Whoever's feet they belonged to, the tracks took a different approach from the way I had gone, and they led right up to the crater's rim.

I shuffled as quickly as I could with the gravel shifting under my feet. I followed the footprints. This was steep, but not as steep as the first route I had tried. Suddenly, I was there, peering over the edge, into a giant cauldron, about 50 feet across, 30 feet deep.

The crater did not contain the gurgling red-hot lava I envisioned. It was filled in with the same gravel that made up the rest of the mountain. That was what Katrina had meant when she talked about going inside of it. I let myself go, sliding into the mouth of the volcano. The walls curled up around me like an earthen womb.

For the first time since arriving in Iceland, the land felt warm and peaceful. A gentle heat rose from the gravel. This was the only outdoor place on the island with no wind. I felt connected to the earth in a way I never had before.

I laid down on my back, closed my eyes, and felt the planet's warmth radiating through my jacket. I tried to relax my breathing, tried to soak in some inner peace. I wanted to meditate.

A Buddhist monk once told me the key to meditation for beginners was to try to empty your mind, but to not fight any thoughts that might creep in. "Think of your thoughts as clouds," the monk said. "Let them come, and let them go."

I tried to focus on my breathing *"Inhale.... Exhale,"* I said to myself.

Like clouds, thoughts appeared on my mind's horizon. "The wind is blowing above me.... *Inhale....* I am warm and safe here.... *Exhale....* I am lying in a volcano.... *Inhale....* This volcano connects to the center of the earth.... *Exhale....* I am one with the planet.... *Inhale....* I am one with nature.... *Exhale....* My boat is about to leave.... *Inhale....* My boat is about to leave without me.... *Exhale....* I have left all of my possessions with a group of drunken strangers.... *Inhale....* They have my camera, which I cannot afford to replace.... *Exhale....* What the hell am I doing inside a volcano? ... *Inhale....* Open your fucking eyes, you dork. The boat is leaving.... *Gulp....*"

One with nature? I needed to be one with my backpack. I leapt up and scrambled down the volcano. I could see the harbor in the distance. The boat was there. Passengers were boarding. I looked at my watch as I ran. I had three minutes.

I made it. Katrine was waiting at the gangway with my bag. She offered me chocolate. That, and the retrieval of my backpack, were inner peace enough.

The seas were calmer on the way back to Iceland's main island. I went out on deck with the Danes, taking in the scenery. We sailed past another little island inhabited only by birds. Suddenly, Laila shrieked. "PUFFFIIIIINNNN!!!!"

I looked into the sea. There it was – a pudgy bird, looking very annoyed. "Damn tourists," the puffin appeared to be thinking. "Must you be so loud?"

He rolled his eyes at us and flew off in search of fish, and perhaps a late afternoon beer.

ANOTHER ANNOYING DISCLAIMER ABOUT BOOZE AND CULTURAL SENSITIVITY

COWERING UNDER A BAR STOOL

T he chapter you are about to read is about the Samis – the indigenous people of far-northern Scandinavia. They come from the extreme fringes of northern Norway, Sweden, Finland, and Russia. For centuries, many Samis lived as nomadic reindeer herders, eking out an existence on a harsh scrap of planet despite brutal winters and even more brutal discrimination. At low points in their history, governments attempted to ban the Sami language, squelch their traditional religion, and steal their land.

In the second half of the 20th century, the Samis started making a remarkable cultural and political comeback. Harnessing modern media, they lobbied for equal rights, a movement that came to a boil in 1979 when a group of Sami activists went on a hunger strike outside the Norwegian Parliament building in Oslo.

Norway's government was planning to build a hydroelectric plant along the Alta River, a move that would have flooded an entire Sami village and displaced several hundred residents. As you can imagine, people whose homes would soon be under water were not amused. They lodged vocal protests that ultimately spared the village and led to new recognition of Sami rights and cultural autonomy.

Ten years after the so-called "Battle of the Alta River," I traveled to Karasjok, one of several large Sami settlements in northern Norway. I spent several days there, interviewing residents and learning all I could about Sami culture. When I returned to America, I turned my notes into freelance newspaper articles, college term papers, and a chapter for a book about indigenous peoples.

The chapter you are about to read in this book is not any of those things.

What I didn't get to write in any of my newspaper articles, college term papers, or educational book chapters was about what happened to *me* in Karasjok. Those earlier compositions were about the Samis. *This* book is about me. *Me! Me! Me!*

What did I do during my several days in Karasjok when I wasn't busy interviewing people? I drank some beer, got molested by a dentist, overslept, drank some more beer, waged war on insects, fell temporarily in love,* survived a dust storm, and ate some yogurt. I also managed to squeeze in a shower.

*not with the dentist

I wrote about all of this in the first edition of this book. After it was published, a couple of concerned readers stepped forth and expressed concern. "You make the Samis sound like a bunch of drunks," they said.

This feedback concerned me. The Samis are not a bunch of drunks, and I would never wish to portray them that way. It's just that parts of this next chapter take place in a bar. People in bars drink beer. People who drink beer get drunk. This happens all over the world, not just in remote Arctic villages.

Sufficiently concerned about negative stereotyping, when the second edition of this book went to press, I considered deleting this chapter. But then I thought, that's silly. In other chapters, I write about drunken Danes, drunken Canadians, drunken New Zealanders, and pot-smoking Turks. None of these references to intoxicated people has come under scrutiny, but as soon as a writer puts a literary beer in the hand of a minority group, people squirm. And if you read carefully, you'll notice this chapter actually includes more sober people than drunk people.

So let's just be clear: Some Samis, like other Europeans, like to drink beer. Other Samis, like other Europeans, do not like to drink beer. I like to drink beer, so sometimes I hang out with other people who like to drink beer. I'm all for political correctness to a certain extent, but denying a couple of beer-drinking Samis their place in this book alongside other beer-drinking Europeans seems somehow racist in a different way. So the chapter's staying.

The following chapter is not an anthropological study, nor is it intended to show an accurate cross-section of Sami society. It's a story about me, at age 20, having a few beers with some people I thought sounded interesting.

Now, if you would like, go get yourself another beer of your own, or another apple juice, and come with me. But whatever you do, beware of the dentist.

NORTH OF DARKNESS

KARASJOK, NORWAY

My cabin was bouncing – boom, boom, boom – up and down in time with the sound system, which was cranked full throttle at the disco across the dirt road. The mosquitoes that had died and fallen to the floor were vibrating in time with the bass. Those that had not yet died looked like they had severe migraines.

This wasn't the scene I expected at a remote outpost, 250 miles north of the Arctic Circle. I'm not sure what I *had* expected. Mosquitoes, probably, but not dead, break-dancing ones. My cabin was part of the Karasjok Youth Hostel. It had two rooms – a main sitting area that served as a living room and kitchen, and a small bedroom with two sets of bunk beds. Toilets and showers were in a building down the hill. The price for a bed was around nine US dollars a night. On this night, I had the cabin to myself.

I had arrived in Karasjok a few hours earlier. My first mission had been to track down food and a mosquito coil. It was 1 a.m. now. I had eaten. I had explored the town. I had murdered several hundred insects with a scrap of corrugated cardboard.

I wanted to go to bed now, but between the festivities across the road, the midnight sun brightening my cabin, a cloud of anti-bug smoke, and a smattering of more stoic bugs still buzzing feebly as they gasped their last gasps, sleep wasn't going to happen. I wasn't in the mood to wander alone into an Arctic redneck bar, but I figured the company in the pub would be more pleasant than the mosquitoes. Besides, I had interviews to track down in the morning. Maybe I'd meet someone who could help. I inhaled one last hit of mosquito coil fumes and crossed the road to the noise.

A short line extended out the door of the building. The building served several purposes. It was a restaurant and bar, a disco, and the office for the Karasjok youth hostel. I took my place in line behind a weather-beaten woman – late 40s, I guessed. Her skin looked like the dry, cracked leather on a pair of shoes ready to be donated to Goodwill. She had salt and pepper hair and a cigarette burn in her voice.

"From where do you come?" she asked me.

Her English threw me. I hadn't expected to hear my native tongue up here. I guessed she was staying at the hostel. German, maybe.

"What?" I said. "Sorry."

"You are sorry?" she said. "For what? Are you an English-man?"

"I'm from the United States. Where are you from?"

"I'm from here," she said. "Karasjok."

"Oh. *Jeg snakker norsk.*"

"I don't speak Norwegian," the woman said.

That made no sense to me. "You live in Karasjok and you don't speak Norwegian?"

She blurted her answer in a language I'd only heard on televi-sion. All I could catch was the prefix on the first word. *Sámi....*

"Oh," I said, surprised. "You're Sami?"

My reaction was like meeting someone in Tokyo and freaking out that they were Japanese. Ninety percent of Karasjok's popula-tion was Sami. They were the reason I had come here. They were a little shorter than mainstream Norwegians, with slightly darker pigments, but their physical appearance wasn't so different that they stood out. I had rolled into town, oblivious that these people – people I had written papers about in Anthropology 101 – were not only real, but surrounding me now. They had taken a mythical place in my mind, like characters from an Arctic fairy tale. I had finally arrived on their turf, surprised they really existed.

"I'm the dentist here," the woman said with an air of importance.

"Really?"

"Yes. Would you like a sweet?" She spoke in a voice I now realized wasn't just accented but slurred from booze. She retrieved a bag of cough drops from her pocket.

"No thanks," I said. I'd been taught not to accept candy from strange dentists.

"Why not? You don't like them?"

"Not right now."

We moved into the entryway. I felt self-conscious being seen with a stumbling drunk woman twice my age. I wanted to go back to the cabin. I was starting to miss my mosquitoes.

She put her arm around me. "Do you like to dance?"

I took her arm off of me. "No thanks."

She put her arm around me again. "What's wrong? You don't like to dance?" She started swaying back and forth, trying to get me to sway with her.

"No!" I said.

Just as I was starting to panic, a friend of hers walked over – a man nearly as drunk as she was. He distracted her for a split second, long enough for me to wriggle free and dart inside to the bar.

It was a dark, smoky place. Thick velvet curtains blocked the midnight sun. I was relieved to see the place was packed. I could lose myself. There was no place to sit, however. Everybody else knew everybody else, and I felt out of place. But I was in now. I'd slurp my way through one beer, then head back.

"Can I have a half liter?" I yelled above the music to the bartender.

"We just stopped serving."

Stopped serving? I had just risked dental molestation for this beer.

The bartender wasn't flinching. "Sorry," he said. "Come back tomorrow."

As I tried to sneak outside, the dentist spotted me. "There you are, my American friend! Where did you go?"

"I have to leave," I said.

"Come dance with me!" She grabbed me again.

"I can't! I have to go!"

We were struggling now. It was becoming an all-out physical altercation.

"Oh, come," she slurred. "It's nice to dance."

I broke loose from her death grip and darted for the exit.

Shaking, I broke into a sprint – up the hill, don't look back. I got to my cabin and fumbled with my keys. "Shit," I mumbled. The lock had been sticking earlier. It was one of those key holes that had to be jiggled just right, not an easy thing to do with a woman my mother's age wanting to drag me off to dance, and probably perform other unmentionable dental acts. I was afraid to turn around to see if she was in pursuit. Eye contact would make things worse. *"Wheep wheep wheep wheep,"* went the stalker movie music in my head.

And then, just like in the movies, just as the scary monster was about to pounce, inches away from the young and naïve victim, I made it inside and slammed the door behind me. I collapsed, breathless, uncomfortably sober, onto the wood floor. I laid there for a moment trying to catch my breath amid a thousand mosquito corpses.

The dentist was nowhere to be seen when I awoke in the morning. The mosquitoes, on the other hand, were up early.

I had never seen so many mosquitoes. They weren't particularly big, but they were bad-assed. They traveled in swarms. They chased me as I walked toward town. The weather was downright bizarre for this part of the planet. Mother Nature had a fever, sending temperatures to nearly 90 degrees Fahrenheit. In spite of the heat, I wore long pants and a jacket. They were my only protection from the bugs, who feasted on my face and hands. Every so often, I'd break into a run and try to lose them. I'd turn to see the cloud of bugs behind me, following me like Alfred Hitchcock's birds.

Wheep wheep wheep wheep....

I found my way to SamiRadio. I had sent them a letter from Wisconsin to warn them I was coming. Once a fledgling local station, SamiRadio had grown into an important special-interest network that broadcast several hours of Sami language programming each day throughout northern Norway, Sweden, and Finland. They were also on the air in Oslo, where a sizeable Sami population had settled.

I spoke with two of their top journalists about how the Samis had harnessed the media in modern decades to reverse the discrimination they had faced. They hadn't just launched a radio network. They had made inroads into mainstream Norwegian television, and even partnered with Disney to produce *The Pathfinder*, an old Sami folk legend that had received international acclaim and nearly scored Best Foreign Film at the Oscars.

(Do not confuse the 1987 version of *The Pathfinder* with the 2007 pseudo-remake, in which 20th Century Fox moves everything to North America. In the new, corrupted version, a gang of Vikings in desperate need of anger management counseling cruises across the Atlantic to slash the heads off of American Indians, apparently because there were no heads closer to home that they could slash off. Then in the end, a wholesome, white Viking boy ends up saving the weaker, indigenous people. Nice going, Hollywood. Luckily for the Samis, they never had their culture dragged into this orgy of gratuitous carnage and decapitation. Unluckily for the Samis, 20th Century Fox did not have the decency to change the name of the 2007 film.)

For two and a half hours, the journalists talked to me – about the rise of their network, and their personal experiences with discrimination. For the rest of the day, I wandered in search of other interviews, stopping at the town library and a small museum. I felt excited when I got back to my cabin in the evening. I had a great article in the works. Dinner was bread and cheese with orange juice. Cherry yogurt for dessert.

It was Friday night. The winds were picking up outside, making the lights flicker. Around eight o'clock, there was a rattle in the key hole. The door to my cabin opened.

"Hello," said a long-haired backpacker. An Asian man behind him nodded.

"My name's Grant," the backpacker said. He was from New Zealand.

The Asian man was from Japan. He had a long name I had never heard before. He spoke little English and went straight to bed.

"So what is there to do around here?" Grant asked.

"There's a disco across the road," I said. "That's about it."

I was unhappy at first to have roommates. I'd been backpacking for three weeks now, and an entire cabin to myself was luxury, but as I got to know Grant, I appreciated the company. I told him about my dental emergency the night before.

"Well do you want to go for a beer? With two of us there, maybe she'll leave you alone."

Leave me alone? I doubted that, but Grant could at least help peel her off of me. And I'd met some people in town during the day. Maybe I'd bump into them. "Sure," I said.

We crossed the road and ordered beers. All the tables were taken so we stood in the middle of the packed bar. Grant began telling me about his travels, but I was distracted, scanning to see if the dentist was there. That's when my eyes locked with somebody else.

It was the kind of scene that only happens in chick flicks. Shy American tourist spots a beautiful young woman across a crowded room, blah blah blah.... She was painfully cute, with short, curly hair and piercing brown eyes. And at age 20, I was painfully shy. Girls terrified me – even more than dentists and mosquitoes. My tongue seized up at moments like this, rendering me unable to speak any language other than Drool. But I held my eye contact for long enough to show I had noticed. This wasn't my usual behavior. Normally, faced with an attractive woman who seemed attracted to me, I would go find a nice table to hide under.

She started walking toward me.

Damn it! What was I supposed to do? I hated pick-up lines. They were artificial. Cowering under tables was more sincere. But she was moving – in chick-flick-style slow-motion – across a crowded bar to talk to me.

Think think think! Fast! Come up with something! Anything!

But no words were coming to me, other than, "Will you marry me?" I kept my mouth shut and waited for her to talk.

"Are you the guy from Wisconsin?" she asked me in Norwegian.

I'm not sure what sort of opening line I'd been expecting, but that wasn't it.

"Yes," I said.

"Well say hi to Wisconsin for me."

"Okay."

And then she vanished into the crowd.

"Wow," Grant said. "You understood her. I'm impressed."

I stood there dumbfounded.

I translated the conversation for Grant. How did she know I was from Wisconsin? Karasjok was small, but was it so small that word of my presence had permeated the town? Was everyone in the bar staring at the journalist from America?

I looked around the room. No one else seemed to notice me.

"Well she keeps looking at you," Grant said.

"What? Where is she?"

"She's right behind you. About seven or eight meters away."

I didn't dare turn around. She might think I was attracted to her.

"She keeps looking this way," Grant said. "She's definitely checking you out."

"Well I have to talk to her. I've got to find out how she knew I was from Wisconsin. Maybe she's Sami. Maybe I can interview her."

"Uh huh," Grant said. "Interview her." He gulped the last of his beer. "She's still staring at you, Dave. I'm going to bed. Good luck."

I started roaming in search of the girl. I found her crammed into a large booth with eight other people.

"Hi," I said. "My name's Dave."

"I know," she said. "I'm Alise."

She knew? Was she a spy?

"How did you know I was from Wisconsin?"

"I work at SamiRadio. I saw you in the station today. And I saw the letter you sent a couple of months ago. I noticed the Wisconsin address. I was an exchange student in West Bend."

Alise invited me to squish into the booth beside her.

I explained I was in Karasjok working on an article.

"I know," she said.

She told me about her time in Wisconsin. About how she smoked cigarettes and wore a leather jacket there, just like she did in Karasjok. "Everybody there thought I was a *dirt bag*," she said, saying the last two words in English. "But I'm really not like that."

No. She was definitely not a dirt bag.

She told me about growing up Sami, about being fluently tri-lingual.

"I'm amazed how many people here speak Sami as their first language, and also speak flawless Norwegian," I said. "There's not even an accent."

"We have to to survive."

We talked for a long time – about Karasjok and Wisconsin, about our families, about traveling, and working in the media. We were squished tightly into the booth with a bunch of Alise's friends. Surely it was an accident that her index finger was hooked under the inside of my sleeve. I excused myself to go to the bathroom.

A burly guy in a leather jacket walked in as I was standing in front of the urinal.

"How's it going?" he asked.

How's it going? Why do guys ask you that when you're, well, *going*? I zipped and washed my hands. "It's going okay, thanks."

"Lots of people here tonight," he said, still going.

"Ummm, yeah." I tried to keep up with his small talk. "Is it always like this?"

"Sometimes. What are you doing here?" he asked. "You're from Oslo."

His voice had a hint of suspicion. He could tell from my dialect I wasn't a northerner.

"Actually, I'm from the United States," I said.

He zipped. "Bullshit." He stepped toward me. "Don't lie to me."

I wasn't sure whether to feel flattered or terrified. This guy was built like a buffalo. One swift stomp to my head and I'd have to go see the dentist.

I stepped back against the wall and shrugged. "Ummm, I am, actually."

He didn't say anything. He just glared.

"You want to see my passport?"

"You really are American. How come you speak Norwegian?"

I explained.

Next thing I knew, I was surrounded by four guys, all firing questions at me about America. Was it dangerous? What kind of a journalist was I? Did I work for the New York Times?

I answered question after question. Other customers came and went.

"Look," I said, "I'd love to talk more, but could we maybe go back into the bar?"

"That's okay," said the guy who had greeted me at the urinal. "We'll talk later."

When I emerged, Alise introduced me to a friend. "We're moving to a quieter table. Would you like to join us?"

Yes please.

It was past midnight. I bumped the curtain and a ray of sunshine came screaming into my pupils. I looked across the table at Alise. Damn she was cute. She excused herself to go to the bar. I was alone with her friend.

Verbal paralysis set in. "So you live in Karasjok?" was the best I could come up with.

"Yeah."

Yeah? Work with me here.

"Are you from here originally?"

"Yeah."

I was catching a weird vibe. The friend didn't seem to like me.

Alise returned to the table with another guy. She introduced me. I didn't listen to his name.

"I'm the DJ in the disco," he said.

"Cool."

"So I can't sit here long. I have to go change the record in a moment."

"Cool."

He was trying to be friendly, but with the noise in the room, it was hard to hear. He and Alise started having an intense conversation. They were arguing, but I couldn't hear what they were saying.

"I have to go change the music," the guy said to me again. Then he looked at Alise. "Come here for a minute."

They left me alone again with Alise's friend who didn't like me. "That's Alise's boyfriend," she sneered.

"Oh."

Well how was I supposed to know she had a boyfriend? Hell, all I wanted to do was interview her.

Across the room, I could see Alise pushing her way back toward our table.

"Sorry about that," she said as she sat down.

"I hope I'm not causing any problems," I said. "I didn't realize he was your boyfriend."

"No. He's not my boyfriend."

"He's not?" I looked at Alise's friend, confused. Alise looked at her too. She looked pissed.

"He used to be my boyfriend. We broke up last month. He's a loser. Besides, he's moving to Tromsø tomorrow to join the army."

Oh great. Stealing away the girlfriend, the ex-girlfriend, the wish-she-was-still-his-girlfriend, whatever, out from under the nose of a guy who was going off to start his obligatory military service in the morning felt morally wrong.

I wished I had shown up a week later.

"Are you going to be here tomorrow night?" Alise asked.

"Yeah."

"We should get together. There's another bar down the hill you should check out."

"Okay."

"Where are you staying?"

"I'm just up the hill in cabin 10," I said.

"Cool. We'll pick you up tomorrow night at 10. Cabin number 10 at 10 o'clock."

At 1:30, the music stopped and the bar staff started herding people outside. I said good night and wandered across to my cabin. I watched Alise as she walked down the hill. Her male friend of uncertain status was waiting for her, trying to coax her into a taxi. She started to walk away. He chased after her, blocking her, grabbing both of her shoulders. I watched the drama from an obscured distance. In the end, Alise got into the taxi.

I awoke in the morning to an empty cabin. Grant and the Japa-

nese man had caught the first bus out of town. So had a Sea Sami
I was supposed to interview an hour earlier.

Sea Samis, as their name implies, are fishermen. They live in
coastal areas, not Karasjok. I was lucky to meet one here. I had
bumped into Johan at the pub the previous night. He was passing
through town on his way to a wedding in another inland village.

But one of the last things I had removed from my too-heavy
backpack before leaving home was my alarm clock. I had slept past
our arranged interview time, and now, Johan was gone.

Frustrated, I skipped breakfast and my usual morning shower.
I grabbed my notebook and hiked into the town center.

I worked through the day without eating. I met people   from
the Karasjok Reindeer Administration who told me
about the changing technology of herding, and how
the Chernobyl nuclear disaster had dealt a devastating
blow to herders farther south. I chatted with shopkeepers and people out walking. Everyone, it seemed,
had a story about cultural strife, about growing up
perceived as second class citizens because they spoke a
different language, or lived a different lifestyle, or quietly
practiced a nature-based religion that a century earlier the
Norwegian government had tried to destroy. Those who worked in
the reindeer trade still lived as nomads for a few weeks each year,
traveling between an inland house and a coastal house in different
seasons to meet the animals' dietary needs. When you're tending
a flock of a hundred reindeer and the animals need to migrate,
you can't just squish them into the family station wagon and drive
them to the coast. So twice a year, the herders would make their
two-week trek, living in their *goahti* – fur-lined teepee-like structures
they could pack up and move.

This was an ancient culture that had nearly been exterminated.
But in the last two decades, they had used modern technology
to make an incredible comeback. Once, their language had been
banned. Now they had their own schools, their own media, and a
new parliament of sorts that was lobbying for Sami rights.

Over the course of the day, I got some fairly good interviews. But fairly good interviews weren't going to cut it. I needed something more personal. I was annoyed with myself for oversleeping and missing my Sea Sami interview. I had to find something to make up for it. I hiked back to my cabin. The winds were picking up again, replacing the mosquitoes with swirling dust clouds.

"Hey, Wisconsin!"

I heard a voice. It seemed to be coming from the sky. I looked around. I couldn't see anyone. Someone had to be yelling at me though. There weren't many people in Karasjok named Wisconsin.

"Up here!"

Leaning out a window, up in the restaurant above the disco, was the burly guy from the men's room the night before. He and a friend were drinking. I went to say hi.

He spoke English to me now. He spoke it well.

"What are you doing?" he asked.

I told him.

"You should interview me," he said. "I know everything about the Sami people."

I was skeptical. Something about this guy's demeanor made me edgy, but I decided to humor him for a minute or two. I was out of paper except for a little pocket notepad. It would do though. This wouldn't take long.

"I had an interview scheduled with a Sea Sami this morning, but I overslept," I said as I sat down.

"Then you should talk to this man." He pointed to the guy beside him.

"Are you a Sea Sami?" I asked in Norwegian.

"Yes," he answered in English. "But not anymore. I have a bad back and my doctor said I had to quit fishing."

The burly man was named Johnny. His mother was Sami. His father was Norwegian. "But I am all Sami," Johnny said. I asked his age. "Old enough," he said. I guessed mid-20s. The Sea Sami's name was Asle. He was older – maybe 40.

"Do you mind if we speak English?" Asle asked. "We don't get much opportunity to practice."

Johnny ordered another beer. I could tell he had been drinking for a while. "Do you know what the best cure for a hangover is?" he asked.

"What?"

"You scare it away." He took a big slurp.

"Don't you have a worse one later then?"

"If you keep drinking, you keep scaring them away. You just can't stop."

I started asking Asle questions. He had lived on the coast for a long time, but a lot of his relatives were reindeer herders. In 1986, his doctor had advised him to quit fishing, and he had moved to Karasjok. He was working on a medical degree now.

"Do you speak Sami?" I asked him.

"I've learned it. Norwegian is my first language."

Asle had grown up during a dark period in Sami history. Discrimination had been rampant in his childhood, and although both of his parents spoke Sami as their mother tongue, they had stifled their language, raising their son speaking only Norwegian so he wouldn't face the bigotry they had. Asle had friends at school who spoke Sami, though, and he had felt left out. Part of his identity was missing. His friends encouraged him to learn the language. They taught him a little bit, but there was no formal instruction. By age 20, he could no longer stand the cultural vacuum. He realized if he was really going to become fluent in the language, he would have to do something drastic.

He had an elderly uncle who was still a nomadic reindeer herder. The uncle spoke little Norwegian. All Asle needed to do was spend time with his uncle, away from Norwegian speakers. So he moved into the old man's tent for a year and helped tend the reindeer. At times, winter temperatures plunged as low as minus-50.

"We had the dogs to keep us warm on our feet," he laughed. "I never gave up."

Johnny told a very different story. He had been raised bilingually. It would have been easier, he said, if he had only spoken Sami. At school, educators used him. There was no hired interpreter, so his teachers would make him translate for other Sami students. His voice grew louder as he recalled a childhood trauma.

When he was seven, he had broken his leg playing soccer. He had been flown by helicopter to a hospital in a predominantly non-Sami town 150 miles north. Doctors treated him, but when they finished, they wouldn't let him leave.

"There were some old Samis at the hospital who couldn't speak Norwegian. So the doctors made me go around to all of them and translate. Think about that. Making a seven-year-old boy with a broken leg go around a hospital and translate between doctors and old people."

I was starting to understand the edginess, the suspicion I had sensed in this man the night before.

A couple of people at a time, Johnny's friends started trickling into the bar. Most played on his soccer team. They were a rowdy bunch, but they listened as I interviewed Johnny.

Johnny had more recent stories of discrimination too. Two years earlier, while playing a soccer match in a non-Sami town, some of the townspeople – even the mayor – had shouted ethnic slurs at Johnny's predominantly Sami team.

The more Johnny spoke, the angrier he seemed. I scrambled to write his quotes down fast enough. When I ran out of pages on my little flip-pad, I turned it over and continued on the back. This was the interview I had been needing.

"You know," one of Johnny's teammates interrupted, "this man knows magic."

"Oh, really?" I said, expecting a card trick or something.

"Black magic."

I didn't believe him. I figured this guy was testing my gullibility. But Johnny wasn't laughing. "I'm a shaman," he said.

"What do you mean?"

"It's part of the old Sami religion. When players on my team are injured, I take away their pain."

I had learned about Sami spirituality at the radio station the day before. Like most pre-Christian religions in Europe, it was nature-based and polytheistic. The journalists had told me many Samis still practiced their religion privately, but in public, they would insist they were Lutheran.

"I didn't think many people still practiced the old religion," I said to Johnny.

"Lots of people do. But most won't admit it."

"So why are you so talkative about it?"

"I don't give a shit what other people think about me. I am a Boheme. I do what I want. They can't hurt me with their words."

"And you say you're a shaman?"

"Yes. This guy hurt his leg in a match two weeks ago. I made it better for him. You can ask him."

The man nodded.

"Do all the players on your team believe this?"

"Of course they do. I heal them."

I looked around the table. A couple of guys nodded shyly. This topic had struck a nerve and quelled their rowdiness. They were stone-faced now. A lot of them didn't want to speak English, but I could tell they were understanding. And I sensed they wanted me to understand them – to understand I was raised in a culture blind to the benefits of ancient beliefs, a culture of spiritual smugness that valued only modern thinking and wrote off the old, nature-based religions as "backward" without considering there might be lessons to be learned.

"So what sorts of things can you do?" I asked.

"I can give pain. I can stop pain. It's a gift."

Asle jumped in. "Can you stop blood?"

Johnny threw him a strange glance. He didn't answer. He turned back to me. "People are curious, but you must not play with your powers. You must not use them for your own benefit."

A man next to Johnny interrupted. "Do you believe what he is telling you?" he asked me.

"I don't know."

"What do you mean you don't know? You are a journalist."

"Yeah. I'm trying to find out what he believes."

"Sure, but do you believe him? You must have an opinion."

"I don't have an opinion. He's got a right to believe what he wants. I'm not here to judge him. I'm here to write what he tells me."

I was gaining Johnny's trust. These questions from his friend were threatening to unravel the interview.

"You're not a good journalist," the man said.

"How do you know what kind of journalist I am?"

"You say you don't have an opinion. Good journalists have opinions."

Johnny told him to shut up.

"Is there anything else you can do with these powers?" I asked.

"You can take trips without drugs. You can leave your body. The first time I did it, I was terrified. I was looking down at myself from above. But it is wonderful. I do it all the time now."

"How?"

"I meditate."

"How did you get these powers?"

"Everybody has them."

Shaman Tours

"I have them?"

"Everybody has them. But few people know how to use them. You must learn how to use them."

"How did you learn?"

"I studied for several years. You see that man over there?"

Across the room was a thin, elderly man talking to some younger people.

"Yeah."

"He's taught me a lot. There was a man at the beginning of this century. He was the best. His name was Johan Kaaven. He could pick things up without touching them. He could even stop cars from going."

"Can you do anything like that?" I wanted to see a levitation act or something.

"No," he said. He wasn't going to put on a side show.

"So you can give people pain, and you can take it away. And you can leave your body. Is that everything?"

"Well, I can do other things, but I shouldn't tell you."

"Okay."

Asle chimed in. "Dave, what we've told you, it's the truth. You won't find it written anywhere. You have to come here, to the source. You can write what you want. You can take out what you want. But we tell you the truth."

"And what we're telling you," Johnny added, "we wouldn't tell to some other journalist from Oslo or America."

"So why are you telling me?"

"I can tell you care about the Samis. And you try to be Norwegian. You speak the language. You're not just doing this because it's your job. And you speak English to us even though you have to practice your Norwegian. I appreciate that. We don't get to practice our English very often. But if you were older, we probably wouldn't be telling you these things."

I nodded.

"I'll tell you something else. But you must be careful what you write."

"Do you not want me to write this?"

"Be careful."

I didn't know what he meant. His expression was foreboding.

"Okay," I said.

"I can also see the future."

"What can you see?"

"I have seen some very good things. And some very terrible things."

"Like what?"

He wouldn't elaborate.

The next thing I knew, my chair started moving, sliding backward from the table. It wasn't shamanic powers though. It was another burly guy. He was yanking me backward to make room at the table for himself. I looked at the man, annoyed.

"He is one of the best Sea Samis in Norway," Johnny said.

"Really?"

The man didn't say anything. He took a huge slurp from his beer bottle, and let the overflow dribble down his chin.

"He is also one of the best Sami musicians."

"Oh?"

"He plays guitar. And that guy there plays drums."

The drummer was shorter than me, and heavier, with long, greasy hair and a scrawny moustache.

"Do you know what we call him?"

"No."

"Muppet."

"Oh."

"Does he look familiar?"

"Uh, I'm afraid not." Was this guy known in Norway?

"Look at him closely. Doesn't he look like someone you've seen before?"

The drummer was smiling at me, waiting for an answer.

"Sorry," I said.

"Do you know the Muppets?"

And then, it clicked. He looked like Animal, the beasty drummer from *The Muppet Show*.

"Oh, yeah!"

Everyone laughed.

Muppet snatched my notebook away.

"Hey, I need that."

He started writing in it.

"I need that back!" I tried to retrieve it, but he wouldn't give it to me until he was finished.

I looked at what he had written.

"'Muppet' one of the 'SAMI' Musicians came here," he had scrawled, as if I was going to plant it, verbatim, in the middle of my article.

There were about 10 people sitting around, listening at this point. Two hours had passed. They were getting drunker, and I was getting hungrier. I had been so busy, I had forgotten to eat. It was five in the afternoon, and 24 hours had passed since my last meal.

"I am going to fuck a woman tonight," Johnny suddenly announced. "I can feel it."

"You are?"

"Yes. I'm ugly. But I make up for it in charm."

A waitress walked out from behind the bar.

"Hilde," Johnny shouted to her, "Do you want to go to bed with me?"

She started yelling at the whole group. Something about the bathroom. They erupted in laughter.

Johnny noticed I wasn't laughing. "Did you understand that?" he asked.

"Not all of it."

"Somebody's been shitting in the *pissoir*. You know what *pissoir* means?"

"Yeah."

"Somebody's been shitting in it."

The group started laughing all over again.

Muppet grabbed my notebook again.

"Give me that!"

He scribbled something in it and gave it back. I opened it up to see what he had written. "PISSOIR," it said.

My interview was deteriorating. It was time to go.

Back in my cabin, I went on a rampage. A fresh herd of mosquitoes had infiltrated my abode. Whacking them helped me burn off pent-up energy. My mind was racing. I had a solid story now, *and* the cutest girl in Karasjok wanted to drink beer with me tonight. I walked down the hill to the communal restroom to shower and shave off six days of stubble. I had been planning to let my beard grow, but that was before I had fallen in love.

With time to kill, I wrote postcards. I updated my journal, and reviewed my budget. I went to the hostel office to tell them I'd be leaving in the morning. Several hours had passed since I left the restaurant. Johnny was finally on his way out.

"I'm going to Finland," he said. A car was waiting outside.

"What are you going to do there?"

"I will drink and fuck."

"Oh. Well, good luck."

"I don't need luck. I have charm."

I went back to the cabin. It was 9:30. Alise would arrive in a half hour. I was pacing now.

The disco across the way was starting to rock again. The sun glowed bright orange, burning through the dust the wind had kicked up earlier.

Ten o'clock came. Then 10:15. I stared out the window until 10:45. An hour after that, I went to bed. I had been stood up.

I caught a bus out of town in the morning, to Hammerfest, the northernmost city in Europe. From there, I could hop a ferry down to Bodø and start the long journey south, out of Scandinavia, into central and southern Europe.

Riding into Hammerfest, I spotted my first wild reindeer of the journey. There were five of them – brown, cuddly-looking beasts with fuzzy antlers, walking single file down the street as if they were out for a Sunday stroll. They shuffled past a bus stop. The people at the bus stop hardly seemed to notice.

A week later, as I recounted my Karasjok story to friends in Switzerland, the town's fairytale status had returned to my mind. It was a place so far away from my own reality in so many ways, I felt as if the journey had been a dream.

But it wasn't a dream. Karasjok is real. I know it exists only because I see it on weather reports when I visit my high school host family down south in Drøbak. That, and my interview notes, are my only tangible proof it isn't fictitious.

I never did hear from Alise again, though I must admit that 18 years later, I've still got an unrequited crush on her.

I wonder if the dentist still feels the same about me.

Temporary Infinity

SWITZERLAND - ITALY - YUGOSLAVIA - GREECE

I awoke with a spike in my head. At least that's how it felt – as if someone had taken a chisel and gently hammered it into my skull. I couldn't see straight. My bed was spinning. I wanted to vomit.

I blinked hard a couple of times and looked around the sleeper compartment. Where was everybody? The train had reached its final destination. Everybody had disembarked. I was lying in my couchette berth, naked, save for my boxer shorts.

My money belt was gone. My money belt, which contained my railpass, my passport, my travelers' checks, my plane ticket home. My backpack was gone too. My clothes, my camera, and all of my work – two months of interview notes and journals.

I had been gassed and robbed. This was the end of my journey. But how was I going to get home with no money, no travel documents, and no clothes?

None of this had actually happened to me...yet. But it was going to if I took an overnight train through Italy. I'd heard the story over and over. It was the Mafia. Or the Gypsies. Or space critters from Planet Zloog. They had a few different tactics. They'd either befriend you and offer you food or drink laced with sedatives, or they'd wait till you fell asleep and smother you with an ether-soaked rag. Or, if they were in cahoots with the conductor, they'd just zap the entire compartment with sleeping gas. Then they'd rob you of everything. You'd awaken 16 hours later, severely disoriented, groping to remove the spike from your head, wondering how you were going to find help in your current state of undress.

"Is it really that bad?" I asked my grandmother's cousin as we ate lunch in Geneva. She lived here. She could separate fact from urban legend.

"Well," she said, "you just have to be careful."

"What do you mean?"

"Don't sleep."

"But it's an overnight train."

"Well, at least keep your important documents somewhere on your body where they won't find them."

I had heard the same night train horror story from too many sources. I'd heard it at a college travel workshop. I'd heard it from a former *New York Times* editor. I'd heard a firsthand variation from an American in France. A week earlier in Spain, he had sacked out for the night on a park bench. He had awoken the following afternoon, groping to remove the spike. His passport, his money, everything was gone. So I couldn't help but feel paranoid. I was starting to think Italy was a land best avoided.

The country was in my way though. I was trying to get from Geneva to Athens. My Eurailpass would cover my travel through Italy, south to the port of Brindisi, and then across the Adriatic Sea on the ferry to Patras, Greece. The only other route was via Yugoslavia. Yugoslavia was reputed to be safer. It was still one cohesive country. But Yugoslavia was in Eastern Europe, and in 1989, the Eurailpass didn't cover travel there.

I had ignored the rumors up to now because I hadn't had to deal with them. But in the morning, one way or another, I was heading south.

"Seriously," I asked my new-found relative, "how often does this happen?"

"It happened just a couple of weeks ago near Venice. They sprayed a sleeping compartment, and when the people woke up, everything was gone."

"Maybe I should go through Yugoslavia. It will be expensive, but it sounds safer."

"No, go through Italy. It will be good for you. How old are you?"

"Twenty."

"Go through Italy. It will toughen you up."

I didn't want to be toughened up. I was perfectly happy with my meek and paranoid self, and I was struggling to see the cultural value in getting mugged.

I decided to go to the source, somebody who would know for sure.

"I have heard the stories," I said, struggling to speak my broken French to the ticket agent, "about the...*euh*...about the Italian trains of the night. Do you know, is it true? About the, ummm, the bad people on the Italian trains of the night?"

"*Mon Dieu!* You have not been listening to those silly rumors, have you?"

That's what I hoped he'd say – that everything in Italy would be just fine. But that's not what he said.

"In northern Italy, it's safe. South of Venice, it gets dangerous. I have friends who were gassed there just a couple of months ago."

I wasn't sure I was understanding his French. I wanted to be misunderstanding. "You know of the people to whom this has happened?"

"Yes. Some friends."

I cringed. "I must think," I said. "I return, please. One moment."

My mind was made up before I was out the door though. A ticket through Yugoslavia would gobble up three days of my budget, but it seemed better than a spike in the head. Besides, even if I did get lucky in Italy and score a ticket in the no gassing section, my neurosis about the issue would trigger a nervous breakdown before Rome. I went back inside and paid for my ride through Yugoslavia.

My journey began with a nine-hour ride to Venice, a city I did not know at the time would later become one of my favorite places anywhere, a city where I would one day feel not only safe, but energized, roaming back streets alone late at night. Right now, however, my mind was swimming with sinister travel gossip.

I had an hour to change trains, eat ice cream, and dodge the Mafia. The Mafia were nowhere to be seen, however. Maybe the train robbers were on strike. I found an ice cream stand and asked for a chocolate and pistachio cone. I sniffed at it. I couldn't smell any sleeping gas. I decided it was safe to eat.

chocolate
pistachio
sleeping gas
caramel crunch

My next train ride, the schedule said, would take 38 hours. I'd cross the Italy-Yugoslavia border in a couple of hours, roll through Yugoslavia overnight and all day the next day, cross the Greek border late the second night, and arrive in Athens around 8 a.m. on day three. I wandered through the station in search of my train.

An international sprawl of rail cars stretched out in front of me – Italian, Yugoslavian, Greek, Soviet, German, all shunted together for the same long journey. I pushed through the aisle, tripping over a group of travelers who had commandeered a patch of floor and set up a barricade with their luggage. They gave me a dirty look. I tried to give them a dirty look back, but it's hard to look intimidating when you've just knocked over somebody else's bags, only managing to maintain your own backpack-challenged balance by flailing your arms and crashing into the guy in front of you.

These passengers weren't the 20-something backpackers from the West that I was used to. They were older, dressed in threadbare formal wear. I was not one of them.

I found my sleeping compartment and peeked inside. There were three guys, all about my age. They blinked at me, looking as apprehensive as I felt. I tried my usual introduction in situations such as this. "English? *Français? Norsk?*"

"English," one of them barked in a South London accent.

"I'm Dave," I said.

"Jamie."

I looked at the guy next to him.

"Jim."

There was an uneasy pause before the last one said his name.

"John."

Jamie, Jim, and John. The Three J's. Cute.

Our compartment was Yugoslavian, but it looked like any West European sleeper – two sets of berths stacked three high, and straps that hung from the ceiling like vertical seat belts to keep you from falling out. The middle bunks folded up against the wall, so the lower bunks doubled as seats in daytime. There were only four of us in this six-person compartment, but with our bags overflowing the limited shelf space and cluttering the floor, it already felt cramped. If anybody else showed up, we'd be doing a painful contortionist act for the next 38 hours.

We sat and got acquainted. We waited to leave. It was time to go, but we weren't moving. "I wonder what's wrong," I said.

Jamie looked up from his train schedule. "This train is rumored to be 10 hours late sometimes. I've heard all kinds of horror stories."

Ten hours? It was too painful to think about. I tried to visualize the length of rail that stretched into the distance. It was like trying to comprehend infinity. Once upon a time, people had hammered all of these rails into the ground, one short track at a time. The fact that they ran uninterrupted, all the way to Greece without a single break, was mind-boggling.

An hour behind schedule, we started moving, traveling until we reached Trieste – the last station on the Italian side of the border. There was a short stop here to hop out and peruse the train station snack bar.

Eating on this journey hadn't crossed my mind. All I had was a little tin of honey and an almost empty jar of Norwegian peanut butter I had carried since Karasjok. I bought a ham and cheese sandwich, some cookies, and a bottle of fizzy water. That would get me through this night. I'd worry about tomorrow's food later.

Darkness fell. There was a short chug to the Yugoslav border where we stopped on an empty, unlit stretch of track. I could see the border police approaching on foot, silhouetted in the bobbing glow of each other's flashlights. A nervous hush settled over the passengers.

Uniformed men spread out to cover the length of the train, boarding and moving slowly through the cars as they did their search. I was going into the East again, into a part of Europe the US government still considered evil.

There were two sounds. Crickets sang in the distance, and doors thudded on their frames as the soldiers flung them open and shut. The crickets' mating call sounded soothing after the drone of train engines all day, but the slamming of the doors broke the stillness. We sat and listened for 30 minutes before anyone came to our compartment.

Jim and Jamie were nervous. They were traveling with temporary passports the British government had issued in the crunch of the tourist season. Printed inside the cardboard documents was a list of countries that recognized the papers. Yugoslavia was not on the list. The soldier didn't seem to care though. He took a cursory glance at our passports, then moved on to the next compartment.

A second soldier came and repeated the process. "British?" he asked Jamie.

"Yes," Jamie said.

"British?" he asked Jim.

"Yes."

"All British," the soldier announced, and then he left us.

Two more officers showed up, also under the guise of checking our tickets and passports, but none of them actually read our documents. I could have replaced my passport photo with a picture of a rooster, and they wouldn't have noticed.

Sufficiently scrutinized, we began rolling again, playing cards and sharing food until we were all lulled into a drowsy, uninterested state around midnight.

BAM!!

I awoke in mid-air as I slammed against the safety straps designed for such situations. I twisted my neck around to see where we were.

The jolt had shaken everyone back into semi-consciousness. "I think we just shunted," Jamie mumbled.

We were in Belgrade. The morning sun was bright. The train was losing a few carriages here. Others from Moscow and Budapest were being added. As we lay in our bunks, railroad workers outside untangled the train cars, shunting (*BAM!*), unshunting (*CRASH!*), switching tracks (*WAKE UP!*), over and over, until the puzzle was complete. Two hours later, we were moving again.

Just as I decided it was time to get out of bed for the day, a ragged couple appeared in the aisle. They had boarded in Belgrade. The man was carrying two car tires under his right arm, strapped together with green twine. His wife struggled behind him with a Black and Decker Roto-Weeder. They plopped their items down in the aisle, along with two large suitcases, and invited themselves into our quarters.

"I have carried these things all the way from London," the man said with a choppy accent. "Please, can you make room for my wife so she can sit?"

Jamie and I looked at each other. Did we have a choice? We'd made it through the first night, just the four of us. Were these newcomers going all the way to Athens? Things were about to get cramped.

The man opened a tin of hideous looking fish stuff and ate it on slices of white bread. Hungry as I was, I hoped he wouldn't offer me any. He began to tell his story. His name was Sokol. He was an English teacher from Bulgaria. He was on the way home from his first trip outside the Eastern Bloc. He and his wife, Nana, had just spent three weeks in London.

The tires were for their Fiat. Western cars were available in Bulgaria. Spare parts were not. The tires he had been driving on were bald, he said, and he couldn't get new ones where he lived.

The Roto-Weeder? I didn't ask.

"London to Bulgaria," I said, "that's a long train ride."

"Yes. We are very tired."

"How many more hours do you have?"

Sokol laughed. "We have been traveling so long, I don't know anymore."

Jamie was looking impatient. My polite tiptoeing around the real issue was getting us nowhere. "Are you going all the way to Athens?" he blurted out.

"No," Sokol said. "We go home to Bulgaria now."

"So how long will you be on this train?"

"We will change trains in Niš."

We still didn't have our answer. Jamie cut to the real question. "Are you sleeping here tonight?"

"No," Sokol said. "We come to Niš in four hours."

Suddenly, their presence was welcome. As long as they took up space, nobody wanting to spend the night would infiltrate our compartment.

"You are from England?" Sokol asked.

"They are. I'm American," I said.

"You are American? From where do you come?"

I didn't know anymore. I was born in California, raised in Maryland. Add a year in England, a year in Norway, and two years in Wisconsin. I had no clue where I came from. "Wisconsin," I said.

"Wisconsin?" Sokol asked. "What state is it in?"

"It's near Chicago."

"Oh, Chicago. Yes," Sokol said. "I see *Dynasty* on television sometimes. Is it like that in America?"

They told us about Bulgaria – their apartment in Sofia and their vacation house on the Black Sea. They taught us Bulgarian phrases and invited us to call if we were in their neighborhood. When we arrived in Niš, the Three J's and I helped them unload their tires and Roto-Weeder. I was sad to see them go. Nana and Sokol had been a nice diversion.

By mid afternoon, a heavy sun oozed through the windows. It made us lethargic. I stuck my head out for some air, and tears blew straight back across my temples. I was like a shaggy dog riding down the highway. The wind fondled my hair as the train chugged deeper into rural Yugoslavia. The alphabet changed from Roman to Cyrillic. For a long time, there were no people. Just flat, lush fields of corn and sunflowers that ran clear to the skyline.

Eventually, people appeared. Our train was twisting through remote, unexplored, tiny villages. Crumbling stucco houses with brick red rooftops freckled the countryside. There were no paved roads. Only dirt paths, carved out in occasional settlements of maybe a couple of hundred residents. Chubby old women in hand-made dresses rode around on donkey carts. The only other means of transportation was tractors.

In the fields, men hacked at the earth with hand tools. Teen-aged girls ushered cows around on rope leashes. Snatches of lives raced past. I had about seven seconds to take in each one. I wanted to hop off in some random village and explore, but all I could do was stand at the window and watch. Life outside seemed very far away, like a program on public television.

Every so often, our train would stop – not at a station, but on a random swatch of track. We would sit and wait. The first time it happened, I thought we had broken down, but I came to understand why this trip took so much longer than a journey of similar distance in Western Europe would take.

There was only one set of rails for trains in both directions. We

we continue the story of a well-to-do cheese maker in rural Chicago...

were constantly on a head-on collision course with another train. To avert such collisions, there were occasional stretches where the tracks split into two sets of rails. We would sit on one of these pull-offs, waiting for the train in the other direction to go around us. In a country that was poor by Western standards, it was a way to save money. But train times were unpredictable. We never knew if we'd wait three minutes or 30 for the approaching train to pass. Over the course of the day, these waits added hours to our journey.

We rumbled through more realistic sized towns too. Not cities by any means, but they had a sense of organization. There were paved roads with names. There were automobiles. The buildings were of stucco, dirtied by polluted air. Laundry hung from the windows.

We stopped about once an hour at village stations. The benches in the stations were the place for gossip. Men sat, one knee crossed over the other, lazily smoking cigarettes. A group of four young girls trying to catch a glimpse of the people on the train giggled when I turned around to find them watching me reload my camera.

An old man squatted down against a lamp post, and for 10 minutes of his life, I studied him through the window. He wore a blue and white embroidered skull cap. He had wrinkled, yellowish skin. A carefully tailored beard ornamented his face. He was alone, dragging long on a cigarette. He had lived hard and simple, and it showed in the trenches of his skin. I had to have a picture.

I snapped on my zoom lens and waited until he turned away. I didn't want him to see me. I focused, then lowered my camera. I was waiting until just the right moment. Just the right pose, with the smoldering stick of tobacco pinched between his lips. I was afraid he might get up and leave. I was afraid the train might pull out of the station.

And then – *CLICK* – I got him.

The train pulled away. I looked down at my camera.

"Oh, SHIT!"

"What's wrong?" John asked.

"I just changed film. My camera was set at the wrong speed."

A simple mistake had ruined a great picture. But maybe the

photo was overexposed for a reason. My memory flashed back to Hammamet. Some photos just weren't meant to be.

As the sky darkened for the night, our entertainment turned once again to card games and guidebooks. We were running low on food. I shared some sesame crackers and my last bit of honey, which by now had melted into a runny mess.

We pulled into another station at ten to nine. It was no big deal until I saw the sign. The alphabet had changed again. We had just arrived in Thessaloniki, our first stop in Greece. We began celebrating. In the morning, we'd wake up in Athens.

Our celebration was premature, however. We hadn't known there were two stops in Thessaloniki. There was the Thessaloniki border station, a station that was nearly empty, and Thessaloniki Central. As we arrived at the central station, we were greeted with a mob scene – swarms of people clamoring to board.

This felt like a mean trick. We were out of food. There was food for sale in the station. But getting off the train to go buy anything meant for sure we would return to find new roommates. That was probably going to happen anyway. And if anyone had *paid* for sleeping berths, as we had, we were going to have to let them in. But as the train began filling with new passengers, it became clear a lot of people had no reservations. They had booked passage in the cheap seats, hoping to stow away in a sleeper car.

I had learned not to mess around with the cheap seats. My first few night trains, I had forgone the 12-dollar couchette fee to stretch my budget. Each time, I had arrived in the morning too zonked to do anything. It was worth 12 bucks a night for a bed and a pillow. The four of us had each paid for our berths, and we were going to defend our turf against freeloaders. But we were hungry. We needed food.

"Two of us should stay here and keep people out," Jamie announced. "And two of us should go for food." Jamie was the alpha-male among the Three J's. He liked to assert his authority whenever possible. He got on my nerves, but right now, I was see-ing the merits to his pushiness.

I wasn't going to keep anybody out. I was too meek. I did, how-ever, know how to sound out the Greek alphabet, and I knew the cuisine. "I'll go for food," I said. "Who wants to come?"

John and I jumped off the train. It was our first time on solid ground in more than 24 hours. "How much time do we have?" I asked a station porter.

"I don't know."

"Two minutes? An hour?"

"I don't know."

"Do we have time to get some food?"

"I don't know."

"Just go, Dave," John said. "He'll blow his whistle before the train leaves."

We ran.

"What do we want?" I asked John as we jogged toward the kiosks on the other side of the tracks.

"I need a bathroom."

We all needed a bathroom. Everybody on the damn train needed a bathroom. Over the last 24 hours, the toilets had become unbearable. Two cars down from us, waste had backed up into the aisle. All day long, I'd been cursing my aching bowels and praising the fact that I was of the pee-standing gender. But given the crowd in the station, I doubted things would be much better here.

There would be no time to find out. A conductor blew his whistle. John and I reversed direction, foodless. I tried to think positively. Given the current bathroom conditions, not eating was probably wise.

There was chaos in the aisles now. People with reservations were trying to get to their assigned spots. People without reserva-tions were scrounging for unreserved places. John and I wrestled our way back to our compartment. Jamie and Jim were just stand-ing there. This wasn't the way to do things.

"Close the curtains," I ordered. It wasn't like me to take charge like this but somebody needed to. We needed to behave like proper 20-year-old men, and make a big mess. A mess that would look like the mess of six people, not four.

"Give me your sleeping bags," I commanded. I threw them onto the two bottom bunks with some other stuff. We spread everything out in the approximate shape of two human lumps, and covered the lumps with sheets. "Perfect," I said, proud of our decoys. We clicked off the light and jumped into our own beds. I looked down at the bottom bunk across from me.

Our decoys didn't look convincing. They weren't breathing. They weren't snoring. It looked like if there were people under those sheets, they were dead people. Or we had gassed them.

But passengers out in the aisle were peeking through a crack in the curtains and moving on. In the darkness, our trick was working. I started to giggle at our success.

"Shut up!" Jamie hissed.

I tried to compose myself. Tried to play dead. Too late. Our door opened.

It was a young boy, nine or ten years old. *"Ella Elena!"* he called down the aisle. "Come Elena!"

What happened next was one of the great linguistic mysteries of the mind. Several years earlier, I had learned a few words of Greek. I hadn't thought about them in years. But like magic, the one word I needed bubbled to the surface of my brain.

"Okhi! Okhi!" I snapped. "No! No!"

"Okhi," the boy shouted back to Elena, followed by a mouthful of unintelligible garble. He slammed our door and disappeared.

My giggles resumed.

"Shut the fuck up!" Jamie snarled. He threw a book at my head.

8:30 the next morning: The four of us were dozing when there was a knock.

"Sorry to wake you. Can I come in?" It was a girl around our age – blonde hair, purple T-shirt, pamphlets in one hand, a half-finished Amstel Beer in the other.

I rolled over and rubbed my eyes. "Sure."

"I'm Fiona. Are you spending the night in Athens?"

"Uh...yeah."

"If you need a place to stay, have a look at this place." She handed me a pamphlet. "I know you don't want to hear me talk about the place, so I'll let you go back to sleep."

Her lack of a sales pitch disarmed me. "Actually, we do need a place to stay," I offered.

Fiona came from England. She was working for Zorba's, one of dozens of cheap, semi-sanitary hostels in Athens that catered to tight-budgeted backpackers. She was working illegally for 2,000 drachmas a day, plus a bed in a shared room, and bacon and eggs for breakfast. At an exchange rate of 150 drachmas to the dollar, it wasn't a lot of money, but in Athens, it was enough for the young and travel-crazed to survive.

Each morning at five, Fiona would catch the train from Athens to Inoi, the first northbound stop. There, she and a gaggle of touts from competing hostels would wait for the southbound train, drinking a breakfast of beer and *retsina*, a resiny Greek wine. The southbound train was scheduled to arrive in Inoi at 7:30 each morning, though in reality, it could show up anytime between late morning and late afternoon. "This is the earliest I've seen it," she said. "You're lucky."

I didn't feel lucky. I'd had as much of this train as I could take. Sanitation had collapsed. The toilets were clogged with an exotic mix of substances I preferred not to think about. But we were nearly there.

Fiona was offering a bed in a four- to six-person room for 1,200 drachmas a night, or a mattress on the roof for 500. Both housing plans included bacon and eggs each morning, and a shower that occasionally had hot water.

"Would you like some beer?" she asked, waving her bottle under my nose.

"No thanks."

I never drank before getting out of bed.

"You'll probably hear from other people with similar offers," she said. "If you want to come with me, find me on the platform in Athens."

We were nearing the finish line. We began gathering our belongings, repacking our bags and retiring our decoys. We were an hour from our final destination, only an hour behind schedule, which, according to the hostel touts, was a new record. Our locomotive kept chugging with a lethargic groan. The longest train ride of my life was nearly over.

The sound of the wheels on the tracks had become hypnotic. The same rhythm had followed us for two days. *Kachugachug. Kachugachug. I think I can. I think I can. I think I...screeeeeeeech....*

The train came to a stop on a lonely stretch of track.

I sighed. One more stop. One more wait for another train to pass. One last delay. It was better than a head-on collision, I supposed.

The day was heating up and the air was still. We were all sweating and smelly. We sat and waited. Nothing was happening. Forty minutes passed. No train came. What was taking so long?

People started getting out to stretch. The scene outside began to resemble a refugee camp. I stuck my head out the window to see what was up. An Englishman yelled to me from a couple of compartments away. "The engine died. They're bringing another one from Athens."

The engine died? *Now?* For 48 hours, I had endured hunger, sweltering sun, time-consuming bureaucracy, and the world's smokiest non-smoking compartments. My stomach was in knots, thanks to the frightful toilet conditions. I was dreaming of a shower. But now, so

REST IN PIECES

ENGINE 51

Died of valve failure

close to the finish line, we were stranded. Our bacon and eggs in Athens were getting cold.

I remembered my thoughts in Venice two nights earlier – about how trying to visualize the distance ahead had felt like visualizing infinity. Maybe this really *was* infinity. Maybe this journey was never going to end. Or maybe I had been gassed in my sleep after all, and I was having some sort of ether-induced nightmare in which the longer we rolled toward Athens, the farther away the city became.

I started to wish I *had* been gassed. "Come and get me!" I wanted to shout to the train robbers. "Knock me out! Take what you want! Please just put me to sleep until we reach Athens! I can't take any more of this!"

But the robbers were nowhere to be seen. Slackers. I would have to stand around and wait with everybody else, painfully awake, baking in the sun.

Our new engine did eventually arrive, and 51 hours after I left Venice, we pulled into Athens. I felt woozy from the long journey, but my head was spike-free. I found Fiona on the platform and we made our way to Zorba's. I had evaded the bad guys, oblivious to a different sort of trouble ahead.

LANGUAGE LESSONS

ATHENS, GREECE

I was the loser.

This came as no surprise. I was no good at cards.

I can't remember what game we were playing. I'm not sure I even knew at the time what game we were playing. And whatever it was, I did not want to be participating in this game, but there was no socially acceptable way out.

The agreement – not an agreement I had agreed to, but an agreement someone who knew how to play cards had imposed – was that the loser had to escort Rhiannon and Kate across Athens at 2:30 in the morning.

Rhiannon and Kate were young Canadian women, staying at a real hotel across town rather than our 8-dollar-a-night pseudo-hostel. It had been decided among our group of eight Anglophiles in the hostel bar that the safe thing would be for a member of the male species to walk them back to their hotel.

This was all well and good on the outbound journey. Like any big, confusing city, Athens was a potentially dangerous place for two young and naïve Canadian women to be wandering late at night. But it was also a dangerous place for a young and naïve American male who tended to get lost a lot to be wandering alone late at night. I was happy to escort the two back to their home, but I worried I'd never find my way back to the hostel.

"I'll go if someone comes with me," I said.

In the end we decided we would all go. We were already tipsy and sleep deprived. A middle-of-the-night urban hike wasn't going to damage any of us any more than the harm we had already inflicted upon ourselves. The eight of us set off into the smoggy night.

Margaret was American, working a power-internship for a US senator. Pita and Sam were from New Zealand. Pita was Maori – one of New Zealand's indigenous minority. Sam was Pita's girl-friend. Nigel and Carrie were Scottish. I rounded out the group as the American who couldn't play cards.

A few minutes into our journey, we came across a park with a small playground.

Kate and Rhiannon hopped on the swings. Sam and Carrie started seesawing. The other four of us, apparently not dizzy enough yet from the cheap beer at Zorba's, decided to give the merry-go-round a whirl. We would spin for a while. Then we would try to walk. Then we would laugh excited laughs, and stagger around until we fell down, and take turns congratulating each other. Pita and Nigel decided it would be a fun thing to spin Margaret around very very fast. Maybe if they did it fast enough, she would do something fun, like vomit.

So they spun her. I added my arm power, grabbing the rails and giving them a good yank.

"Woooo!" shouted Margaret, because that is what drunken American tourists who are being spun dangerously fast, around and around, in the middle of the night, in Athens, Greece, tend to shout. As the speed increased and the centrifugal force pushed her outward, she struggled to hang on. It seemed she was about to go flying, fast and hard, possibly into a tree, or into one of us, and break an assortment of bones.

"Woooo!" she shouted again.

We spun her and spun her, faster and faster. I began to worry about her safety, but only in an abstract, hypothetical kind of way. Spinning her was more fun than worrying seriously about such issues. So I kept the merry-go-round going round. So did every-body else. I was laughing. Pita and Nigel were laughing. Carrie and Kate and Rhiannon and Sam were all off of their playground contraptions, and they were laughing too. Everyone was watching Margaret. Everyone was laughing. Even Margaret, who was prob-ably about to die, was laughing.

Then, Margaret changed her tune. Suddenly, her primal shrieks of glee began to sound like actual words. Words like, "Oh my God! Oh my God! Stop! Oh my God!"

The rest of us laughed some more. I admit it; I laughed along with them, though in the back of my mind, I was starting to won-der if something might be wrong. Was she going to fall off? Was she going to be sick? No. That wasn't the problem. I turned around to look at the faces of my fellow drunks. That's when I noticed the six guys with machine guns.

They were uniformed – not that it mattered. When six guys are pointing machine guns at you, you do what they say, uniforms or no uniforms. But these guys were police. They were pointing their guns at us, caressing the triggers.

We stopped spinning Margaret.

We looked at the men in uniforms. They looked at us. We looked at their guns. They looked at us looking at their guns. The biggest of them shouted something none of us could understand. This was awkward. We spoke no common language.

Normally in my travels, when faced with a situ-ation where I had to communicate with people I did not share a language with, it didn't intimidate me. I saw us as equals with a common obstacle to tackle, a bridge to build. All it took was creativity and mutual respect. But here's the thing about language bar-riers: If two groups of people do not speak the same lan-guage, and one of those groups has big machine guns, the people with the guns have the upper hand.

After a few moments of mutual staring, one of the gunmen decided to try to bridge the gap between us. "Passport!" he demanded, which I believe might be the Greek word for, "Come have a cultural experience in our prison."

I started to reach for my moneybelt. My passport was stashed inside.

That was probably not the wisest of moves. When six guys are pointing guns at you, reaching for something under your belt can trigger cultural misunderstandings. But they didn't notice me. They were focusing their attention on Pita. Pita was of darker complexion than the rest of us, and that seemed to be of interest to the officers.

"We don't have our passports," Sam said. "They're at our hostel."

I decided that was a good story. I stopped reaching for my moneybelt.

"Where you from?" barked the largest of the officers. He was glaring at Pita.

"New Zealand," Pita answered in his New Zealand accent.

The gunmen stared at him, confused.

"We're from New Zealand," Sam repeated. "He's my boyfriend." Sam was white. She knew race was the issue here, and she was trying to show some solidarity with her Maori partner.

"*Nea Zealandia?*" one of the officers asked. Pita and Sam looked baffled.

"New Zealand," Pita and Sam both said again.

"*Nea Zealandia?*" the largest and apparently most senior of the officers kept asking.

"People," I wanted to say, "here is a linguistic pop quiz: *Nea Zealandia* is the Greek word for: (a) New Zealand, (b) Botswana, (c) Saturn." But instead of speaking up, I lingered on the sidelines, trying to remain inconspicuous.

All eyes were on Pita. This meant they were not on me. I was on the fringes, possibly a safe enough distance to slip away quietly and sprint back to the hostel bar for one last beer before bed. I eyed the bushes that would obscure me from view if I could tiptoe 10 feet without being seen.

I rejected the idea.

"Scotland, New Zealand, America, Canada," Nigel offered.

"Ameriki?" the head honcho was asking, puffing out his chest in a show of "I have a machine gun and you don't" machismo.

"Ne," I finally spoke up. "Yes. *Ameriki.* Canada. Scotland. *Nea Zealandia."*

"Nea Zealandia?" the puffy chested man asked, pointing to Pita.

"Ne. Nea Zealandia."

"Does that mean New Zealand?" Sam blurted in my direction, her voice suddenly filled with innocent curiosity rather than the realization that there were six men pointing machine guns at us.

But before I could answer her, the police officers again started interrogating Pita in Greek.

There was no question the attention on Pita was due to his race, though I believe the officers were concerned with his nationality, not his skin tone. Athens was experiencing a boom of illegal aliens sneaking across the border and making their way to the capital from countries to the south and east. Some of them were working respectable, albeit illegal jobs. Others were dealing drugs or whacking random people over the head and taking charitable donations from their victims' wallets. Greece was struggling to control the tide of illegals. Among the rest of us, Pita stood out. I sensed, however, that if we could just convey to the officers that "New Zealand" was not the English word for, say, Albania or Somalia, they would probably let us all go.

The squabbling continued. The Greeks spoke Greek. The Nea Zealandians spoke English. We needed an interpreter.

Luckily, I spoke Greek.

Well, no. That's not true. I spoke a handful of tourist survival phrases, culled from a phrase book. Unfortunately, "Please don't shoot," was not one of those phrases.

A younger-looking officer was standing off to the side. He had a handsome, gentler face than the head honcho and the other cohorts. He looked only a few years older than me.

Here's a useful travel tip, if you should ever find yourself at a park in the middle of the night, surrounded by angry people with machine guns: Look for the young guy. He's usually the weak link in the chain of thugs.

I took a couple of steps toward him.

"*Parakalo,*" I said, "*Sighnomin.*"

It was the most appropriate phrase book Greek I could muster. "Please. Excuse me." In the moment, it seemed a better choice than "May I please have a beer and a souvlaki?"

The young officer smiled and dug deep in his brain for some English. "Don't worry," he said with a heavy accent.

He tapped the big guy on the shoulder and spoke to him in Greek. I couldn't understand the words, but from his body language, I could make out what he was saying.

"Sir, they're drunk tourists from non-threatening countries. We've made our point. The short one over here who looks like he's about to cry just said he's sorry."

This aroused the head officer's curiosity. He stepped toward me, fingering his trigger.

"*Milate ellinika?*" he barked. "You speak Greek?"

"*Okhi,*" I said. "No." I looked helplessly at my new friend.

"He just said '*sighnomin,*'" the young guy seemed to be saying. "He's learned a little Greek. He's drunk and trembling. Besides, if we shoot them, think of the paperwork."

The big officer eyed us all sternly. He took his finger off his trigger.

"Go to bed!" he bellowed.

We nodded and smiled feeble smiles and backed away apologetically, still watching for any sudden raising of guns. Twenty minutes later, Kate and Rhiannon were safely back at their hotel.

Margaret never did break any bones. Nobody vomited. Kate

and Rhiannon thanked us for the walk. The rest of us returned to Zorba's and celebrated our survival with one final beer.

I learned an important lesson that night: When traveling in foreign countries, it's good to learn a few local phrases before you go. The people with guns will like you better. Sure, all that memorizing might give you a headache, but bullets tend to have a worse effect.

Prostitutes, Drugs, and a Magic Vest

ISTANBUL, TURKEY

I was pissed off at myself and everyone around me.

I was pissed off at the Turks because two of them – two people in a nation of 40-million – had ripped me off. A taxi driver had charged me the night rate in the daytime. A shoe shiner had charged me for a shoeshine I didn't want. Total loss from both scams: about eight US dollars. Two people had conned me out of eight bucks, and as a result, I was throwing a silent tantrum against the entire nation of Turkey.

I was pissed off at myself for thinking the way I was thinking. Here I was, dropping into a culture I knew nothing about, whining about how broke I was because my three-month international travel budget was dwindling, hating an entire nation because two unscrupulous residents had just tricked me out of my lunch money. I was a visitor in this crowded city, a city wrestling with poverty like so many crowded cities do. People were doing what they needed to do to survive. If I didn't like it, I could go home. Besides, I had overstayed my welcome. I had made a promise to leave Turkey after four days.

I hadn't made that promise to the Turks. I had made it to myself. When it came to culture shock, Turkey felt out of my league. I'd caught a boat from Greece with a frightened and condescending plan: Get in and out quickly before anything bad happened.

What bad things would befall me if I stayed a fifth day? I wasn't sure, but I had seen *Midnight Express*. I had learned from that movie that Turkey was a crazy place where informants sold you drugs whether you wanted them or not and then turned you into the police, who would torture you in their filth-encrusted prisons until you killed a guard, stole his uniform and keys, and escaped to freedom. Cue theme music. Roll credits. Please dispose of your empty popcorn containers as you exit the lobby.

That was all I knew of Turkey. It was an "exotic" place, a place not to linger too long if you wanted to get out alive.

On day one in Istanbul, my suspicions that Turkey was not like America were confirmed by the bear in the street. The bear was hanging out with a human, who led the bear around on a leash. For a buck or two, you could pose next to the bear and have your picture taken while the bear mauled you.

On day two, I got mauled repeatedly. Not by the bear. By shoe shiners. I feared them more than I feared the bear. They accosted me on the street, got in my way, told me my shoes were ugly. When they did this, I would panic and run. I didn't stop to ponder that actually, my shoes *were* ugly. I'd been traveling in them since late May. It was August now. I had climbed volcanoes, fallen in fjords, and basically obliterated the shoe polish. But I was determined not to have my shoes shined. They were a record of my wanderings.

On day three, my attitude started to change. That's the day I learned how to cross the street. Rush hour in central Istanbul lasted from roughly 3 a.m. to midnight. And I'm not talking rush hour in the conventional American sense. Imagine taking all the drivers in America, putting every single one of them in Manhattan, and changing the traffic light rules: Green means honk and go if you can (if you can't go, just honk), yellow means speed up before the light turns red, and red means the jerk in front of you didn't go fast enough so you'd better run the light and honk at him. You should not actually *try* to hit pedestrians. They should get out of your way, *insha'Allah*, but if they did not, and you crunched them, it was God's will.

Save me! The shoe shiners are coming!

On my first couple of days in Istanbul, as a pedestrian, I had been too frightened to cross the street. When my friend Bahadır wasn't around, I stayed within the one-block radius of the youth hostel. On day three, a more experienced traveler had taken me under his wing, and taught me how to cross: Close your eyes and go. It worked. Cars would slow down. They would honk, but they weren't honking at me. They were honking with me. That was just what drivers did in Istanbul.

Once I learned how to cross the street so I could wander, the real Istanbul revealed itself. I discovered that in spite of the way the American media portrayed Turkey, the average Turk was not a terrorist or a police informant. Furthermore, the bear was quite docile. Once I relaxed, I discovered an intoxicating city, bubbling with humanity. And most of those bubbly humans were kind, friendly people who would help me if I asked for help.

On my fourth day, when it occurred to me that not a single person had attempted to throw me in prison or kill me, I decided to stay a few more days.

I was going on two weeks now, falling into a routine. Every morning at sunrise, static would crackle from the loudspeaker atop the minaret across the street, pulling me out of my slumber. The muezzin would sing the day's first call to prayer. *"Allahhu akhbar!* God is great! Come and pray!"* I understood neither the words nor the religion, but there was a passion in the prayer call that energized me. In two weeks, Istanbul had changed from spooky to magical.

"How much longer do you think I should stay?" I asked Bahadır as we ate dinner one night at a shopping mall on the Asian side of the city.

"Another month."

"No, really. I have to be in Norway in three weeks to catch my flight home, and I still want to travel through Eastern Europe."

"Oh," Bahadır said. "Then forget Eastern Europe and stay three more weeks."

He was serious. I had barely scratched the surface of his country. Besides, this trip was about spontaneity, and I had no desire to leave my new favorite country.

"I could see Eastern Europe some other time," I said. "It's not going to change overnight." I was oblivious, like the rest of the world, that the Berlin Wall would topple four months later.

Bahadır convinced me. I would stay in Turkey until it was time to fly home.

So I stayed. Some days I went sightseeing. Others, I just wandered. When Bahadır had time, we hung out, but I was comfortable on my own now.

I'd known Bahadır for three years – sort of. He had been an exchange student at my high school. When he first arrived in Maryland, barely able to speak English, I had interviewed him for the student newspaper. Suburban Washington, DC, was a lousy place to be an exchange student. Every son and daughter of every ambassador, diplomat, and World Bank official lived in the Washington suburbs. Being foreign was nothing special. If you showed up struggling with your English, you were exiled to the English-as-a-Second-Language clique. Throughout the year, I would pass Bahadır in the hallway and notice his English improving. I had wanted to get to know him, but I'd been too shy.

It wasn't until after I moved to Norway, started going through the same struggles he had encountered in America, that I started to comprehend what he had been through. We became sporadic pen pals. Then, out of the blue, just as I was getting ready to leave Madison on my current journey, he had sent me a postcard. "You have an open invitation to visit Turkey."

People make those invitations. They don't expect you to come knocking, halfway around the planet, two months later. But here I was. Had it not been for Bahadır, I wouldn't have come to Turkey.

For nearly three months, I'd been traveling rough, sleeping in hostels, on trains, on beaches and train station floors. I had subsisted on so many scrawny meals of bread and cheese, I could barely stand the stuff anymore, but the adventures kept me choking it down.

I had the flu now. I'd had it a week. It began as a sore throat. Then came the cough, the stuffy nose, the aches and fever. I had traveled hard, on a crazy-tight budget, overland from the northern tip of Norway all the way to southern Turkey, My body was now telling me it had its limits. Each day, my fever would bump a few tenths of a degree higher, but I tried to keep going. Finally, on day 16 of my four-day Turkish blitz, I realized it was really time to go. I was seriously ill, and probably not going to be healthy until I found more stable surroundings. The next morning, I caught a taxi across town to the Turkish Airlines office.

I sensed right away something wasn't right about the taxi driver. He was too friendly. But I was too polite to question what I suspected, that the word *gece* on the taxi meter meant he was charging me the "night" rate at 11 in the morning. Then in the afternoon, a kid had cornered me on the street, flinging a glob of polish onto my shoe before I could stop him. I'd been determined to get through Turkey without a shoe shine. I liked the volcano scrapes, the fjord-weakened stitches, the burn marks and wine stains. But the kid was shining them up before I knew what hit me. Then when he demanded payment, I obliged.

I felt violated. And feverish and cranky. My nerves were frazzled. I arrived back at the youth hostel with a plane ticket out of there the next day. I decided to spend my final hours holed up in the hostel courtyard, a sterile, non-Turkish oasis, where other travelers would listen to me whine about my sore throat and my day's misfortune. That was my plan. There was just one thing I needed to do first. I wanted a shirt.

I had seen these shirts hanging in shops. They were cotton, with a gray or white base, and colored lines that faded in and out in bright but gentle hues. The coloring process vaguely resembled batik, but the straight, vertical lines, and the buttons and collars, gave them an almost formal look. I had never seen anything like them. I liked them enough to brave the chaos one last time.

Halfway to the Grand Bazaar, though, I changed my mind. I'd been through the bazaar a couple of times already. It was a popular tourist attraction, but not for the timid. The carpet sellers there were the most aggressive. They'd get right in your face, trying a mix of jokes, demands, questions, and invitations in any language they could muster to lure you inside. I wasn't in the mood. Instead, I turned down a side street, to a residential neighborhood sheltered from the touristic mess. It was a street of nondescript apartment blocks with no shopkeepers to hassle me. My mind could settle here. I wouldn't have to talk to anybody.

An old man swept the steps in front of his apartment. I studied his face as I approached. His skin was coarse with age, but he looked content. He turned when he heard my footsteps. Striving for invisibility, I cast my eyes down. But in that brief moment, it registered. The man had just smiled. And I had turned away. I looked up at him again. He was watching me. Still smiling. Not the vulturous grin of so many shopkeepers. He had a warm, friendly glow, a look that said, "You look tired, friend."

I forced a smile. His face brightened.

Did he smile at everyone who passed his way, or had I looked sad? I hadn't realized it until now, but beneath my cynicism, beneath my anger at 40 million Turks, and the simultaneous guilt I was laying on myself for thinking so negatively, there was sadness – the kind of sadness born from pure and simple exhaustion. I was burned out. I was starting to crack, silently taking out my frustrations on the people around me.

I forced myself to meet the old man's gaze again. His smile had a no-strings-attached sincerity. I wondered: In my day's paranoia, had I run from the smiles of others?

"Hello," I said shyly, wishing I had learned more Turkish.

He nodded reassuringly. I wanted to hug him.

A few minutes later, I came to a small bazaar. The old man's smile was still resonating in me, and for once, I decided not to be defensive when the sales pitches started. I didn't have thousands of dollars to buy a carpet. I just didn't. So what was I worried these guys were going to do? Dupe me into buying a 3,000-dollar carpet

My carpet: she dices, she slices, she makes coffee!

I didn't want for the 23 dollars in my pocket? What if I chilled out for once and actually talked to them?

A salesman spotted me wandering alone. He ran from his shop and grabbed me. "Hey, man, where are you from? Iceland? I love Iceland!"

I was wearing a T-shirt from the Hard Rock Café in Reykjavík.

"No," I said. "America."

"America? I love America!"

I smiled cynically.

"You want to buy a flying carpet?"

"I can't."

"Come on man!"

He was talking to me like a college pal, attempting to lure me to a party when I needed to study. He wasn't trying to rip me off. He was trying to make a living. His fingers were locked around my arm, ready to pull me inside his shop, but for once in my life, I convinced myself such behavior was harmless.

"I can't carry it. I'm traveling with a backpack."

"We can ship. Anywhere in the world. To America!"

"I don't have any money."

"You have plastic card?"

"No!" I tried to dislodge his fingers from my arm. "I'm sorry. I can't buy a carpet."

"Okay," he said. "What is your name?"

"My name's Dave."

"Welcome to Turkey, Dave. Perhaps when you are older, you have more money. Come to my shop. I sell you a carpet."

"Okay."

I shook his hand and walked on.

That hadn't been so bad. The guy had been pushy, but in past encounters, who had been the unfriendly one? I had snarled at these guys like they were cannibals inviting me to dinner. I didn't snarl this time, and he didn't snarl back when I gave him my final no.

It was time to meet Bahadır for lunch. I went back to the hostel to wait for him. The little shop in the hostel courtyard had clothes for sale. Maybe I'd find my shirt there.

I combed through a rack of vests, colored in the same style as the shirts. There was one that looked okay – gray with orange and pine green. It didn't thrill me though. I could find better.

Bahadır was a tour guide. He had escaped his group long enough to eat with me. We scarfed down several plates of *köfte* – spicy Turkish meatballs. After lunch, we wandered for a while. I stopped at an outdoor stall that sold the kind of shirt I was looking for.

"Oh, you don't want that," Bahadır said. "That's not fashionable."

"What do you mean?"

"That hippie shit?"

"Hippie shit? What are you talking about?"

"Oh, come on," he said, pulling me away.

We walked a little longer until he had to get back to work. I wouldn't see him again until morning.

I started back toward the hostel, wanting a nap. I was still dizzy with fever.

I passed a guy in a hippie shit shirt.

Okay, so maybe they weren't the rage in the Istanbul fashion scene, but I wanted one. I turned toward the market and walked briskly, almost running. Bahadır didn't have to know.

I got less than two blocks when a kid in a leather shop pounced on me.

"Hey man, where are you from?"

I just wanted to buy my shirt and take my nap. "America," I groaned.

"America? Where in America?"

This was a new one. Usually they just said they loved America and tried to sell me something.

"Wisconsin," I said. "Near Chicago."

"Oh yeah," he said, grinning. "I'm from New York, man!"

"You're from New York?" His accent was impressive, but this kid was not a New Yorker.

"Yeah, man. You know Greenwich Village?"
Greenwich Village? How did he know Greenwich Village?
"Yeah."
"White Plains?"
"Look," I said. "Be honest. You're not from New York."
"No." He lowered his eyes in defeat, but he was trying to conceal a smirk.
"But you've lived there?"
"Yes." His face sparkled again and he looked up.
"Your English is great," I said. "How old are you?"
"Fifteen." He took my hand. "Come to my shop."
"No. I don't have any money."
"You don't have to buy anything. Just come talk." He led me up a narrow staircase to the second floor. The pungent scent of leather hit me as we went inside. Jackets and pants, skirts and hats, anything that could be tooled from leather hung on the walls. The room was carpeted with ornate rugs. It appeared to be a family-run place. Three adults chatted in a corner, but they paid no attention to me and the boy. Another tried to sell jackets to a German couple.

The boy brought two glasses of apple tea.
"How long did you live in America?" I asked between sips.
"You want the truth?" he asked.
"Yeah."
He held up his hand, forming a circle with his thumb and index finger. I stared, confused.
"Zero," he said.
"What?"
"I've never been there. How's my accent?"
As skeptical as I was of his claim to be American, I was equally skeptical he had never been there. His English was too good. But it was true. His name was Ali. He had only studied English for four years, but he practiced every chance he got. He had a pen pal in White Plains. He watched American movies, mimicking accents until he mastered them. His dream was to go to America.

He told me about his family, his school, his work in the leather shop. We talked for a half hour or so. As I got up to leave, I told him about the shirt I wanted. He pointed me toward Aǧa Sofia Cathedral. "Behind there, there is a good bazaar."

I passed shops where the day before, I had had to fight off salespersons, and move briskly so as not to show any interest. This afternoon, there was no pressure. I could gaze. I could touch the merchandise. If I wanted help, they'd help me. If I didn't, they'd go away. It was odd. A new and eerie calm had settled over the city. Or was it within myself?

Several blocks later, I found the bazaar. I was about to turn the corner to look for my shirt when I spotted something much more inviting – a small side street – a narrow passageway into unexplored Istanbul. I had no idea where it led. All I knew was there would be no tourists.

I slipped through the gateway. Two boys, maybe eight years old, ran toward me. "Hello, mister!" one shouted.

"Hello," I replied shyly. He came to shake my hand. I held my hand out. But he was waiting for something more. He craned his neck, like he had a secret to whisper. As I leaned down, he kissed me on both cheeks, the way Turkish men greet old friends. His buddy was hanging back a safe distance, laughing hysterically at his boldness. I waved goodbye and walked deeper.

This little neighborhood was perfectly undiscovered – two blocks from the tourist-clogged streets, but so different. Foreigners never bothered to walk here. For more than a week, I'd missed this place. This was the Istanbul I had been looking for. Gray-haired men with bushy mustaches filled the corner tea shop. Pudgy women in head scarves gossiped on the sidewalk. People eyed me suspiciously. It wasn't a hostile suspicion, but bewilderment. I wasn't one of them. Was I lost?

The smiles I'd received earlier were multiplying inside me. If someone stared for more than a moment, I would smile at them. Sometimes, they smiled back.

Apartments stood three or four stories high. Most were a drab cement-gray. Laundry hung from open windows. Some buildings were flaking away, ready for a sneeze to knock them down. This was a poor part of town in a city of 10-million. In America, I thought, I would not feel safe in such a neighborhood. But here I felt very alive.

Down the street, a soccer match was heating up between two packs of kids. I tried to walk around them, but as I passed, they lost interest in the ball. I became their entertainment. Adults were too timid to approach, but the children swarmed around me. Some tested their couple of phrases of English. Others just stared, tagging along for awhile, then retreating.

The streets had no organization. No tidy rows of blocks; just a winding maze that ran like a river where it pleased. I couldn't dive too deep. As much as I wanted to, I couldn't get lost here. The sun was low in the sky. The afternoon prayer call would begin soon. I decided I should start winding my way back to my familiar tourist oasis.

It was 6:30 now. Most of the shops were still open. I had a powerful feeling of peace in this once-intimidating city now. All it had taken was a few smiles and a walk through a quieter neighborhood.

As I entered more familiar territory, my serenity suddenly shattered. I was passing another carpet shop when the owner pounced. He grabbed my shoulders and shook me. "Where you from?!" he demanded.

I blinked, wondering whether to stay and chat or run like hell. He was smaller than me, and spindly. He wore an old, pastel green T-shirt and jeans. His hair was messy. He had a wound up look in his eyes and a scrappy beard. His feet were bare.

"America," I answered, hesitantly.

"America! I love America! Come into my shop!"

"I have no money." I resisted, but he started maneuvering me toward the door.

"You don't have to buy anything! I am Ali! Drink some tea! Sit here!" He nudged me to the ground, onto a rolled up carpet that doubled as a bench. Another guy watched lethargically, curled in the corner.

Was this another scam? Three times in one day?

"Are you crazy?" he asked in a thick accent.

"Am I crazy? No."

"That's too bad. We're crazy. This is my cousin. You want *çay*? Tea?" He was firing questions at me in splintered English faster than I could think.

"Uh, yeah. Sure." I was suspicious, but my curiosity held me there. Ali darted back into the street.

I looked around, trying to assess things. I was by the window. A big, plate glass window on a crowded street. They wouldn't try anything where everyone could see us, would they? The door was wide open. I could run at any time.

Letting my guard down had made my day a lot more pleasant, but I knew not to get complacent. Ali moved fast, asking question after question. My instincts were clashing, but I stayed. Maybe I was about to get nailed again. Or maybe I had just become the guest of honor in a Turkish carpet shop.

It was a small shop – about 10 by 15 feet, dimly lit with a string of lights around the ceiling. Carpets hung from every wall. Some were brand new, others decades old. The room had almost no furniture. Just a small end table that supported a large boom box and a shoebox full of tapes. Def Leppard was blaring.

Ali ran back in and fidgeted with the stereo. He sat down. Jumped up. Walked around the room. Looked out the door. Sat down again.

A small boy appeared with tea and I took my glass.

"You want a cigarette?" Ali offered, extending a packet of Marlboros.

"No thanks," I said. An offer of a smoke was a common gesture of hospitality here – an offer I sometimes accepted out of politeness, even as a non-smoker, but my throat was too sore now.

"You no smoke?"

"Not today."

"But you can have," Ali said. "Please."

"No. Thank you. I have a sore throat."

"You have what?"

"My throat is sore," I said, rubbing my neck. "I am ill."

"Oh," Ali said. "How do you say?" He pointed to his own neck.

"Throat."

"Troat?"

"Yes."

He scrounged the shop for show-and-tell items. His photo album was full of cars and friends. Proudly, he showed me an English paperback – a short play by Shakespeare. "So I can learn better English," he explained.

Next he brought out a Turkish translation of the Bible. "Turkey is a Muslim country," he announced. As if I hadn't noticed the mosques on every corner. "But I got this book from an American man. I'm very interested in the Christian religion. Are you Christian? What are you?"

"Well, it's a bit complicated...."

"No, it's okay. It's okay," he interrupted. "If you're not...or... are you...do you like Christian?... Or...Turkey is a Muslim country.... Do you like music?"

It was an abrupt change of subject only someone speaking a foreign language could get away with.

Over the next hour, Ali's true motive became clear. It was the same reason the younger Ali had befriended me in the leather shop earlier. He wanted to practice his English. He was 20 years old. The shop was his own – a gift from his father. His father was a wealthy man with shops all over Istanbul. He had given this little one to Ali to expose him to the tourist trade. Here, Ali was to speak English with the stream of foreigners who drifted through each day. Next year, Ali said, he would move to America, where he would solidify his English. Then he'd come back to Istanbul to peddle in the Grand Bazaar with the best of them.

"I work very hard," he said. "Sometimes late at night if people come." But work for him was a game. He had fun – hanging out, drinking tea with his friends, dragging in unsuspecting foreigners when he felt up to it. I doubt he knew how much he did for the travelers he accosted. Bringing them in here for an hour to chat did so much more than plopping them on a bus and herding them around the tourist sites.

A heavy set guy appeared at the door, and an excited dialogue began in Turkish. Ali jumped up again and ran outside. Immediately, he ran back in.

"There is a prostitute outside!" he exclaimed. He waited for me to respond.

"Oh."

"I have to fix it for my brother. I am carpet salesman. I am good businessman."

He ran outside again.

He ran back in.

"No, no!" he said. "I am not *peemp*. You must not think I am *peemp*. You know what *peemp* is?"

"Yeah. I know what a pimp is."

"I am not *peemp*. I just fix for my brother. I am better talker."

Through a crack in a curtain that separated the shop from a back room, I could see him washing his face and combing his hair. "You like Turkish girl?" he yelled as he groomed himself.

I froze. Was he asking me if I liked Turkish girls, or if I would like a Turkish girl? Saying no could insult all the women of his country. Saying yes could cause all sorts of other problems. "Yeah," I said without thinking. It seemed the polite response.

"You wait here," he said. He ran outside again.

I sat nervously for several minutes, rehearsing a polite exit. This was a misunderstanding that could get me in trouble. Ali poked his head back in. "Come here," he instructed, and ran back outside before I could clear things up.

I followed, practicing my clarification in my head. Ali was waiting by a large white Cadillac that could only be described as a peemp-mobile. It stood out in Istanbul like a camel in downtown Chicago. The car had tinted windows. I couldn't see inside. "Sit down," Ali said. Then he opened the door for me. The driver's side door.

Was he crazy? I was not going to drive in this city. No way. No prostitutes, and no driving. Those were my two new rules for getting out of Turkey alive in the morning.

I peered into the car to see if there was someone waiting for me. There was not, so I sat down. Only halfway in, mind you. I kept the door open, one foot in the street in case I needed to run. I couldn't figure out why Ali wanted me in the driver's seat.

Ali hopped in the passenger side. "How does this work?" he asked, pointing to the stereo.

"What?"

"I don't understand these things."

A flood of relief washed through me. Ali had just brought me to this car not to sell me a few moments of pleasure, but for an English lesson. Words like "fader" and "graphic equalizer" – what did they mean?

A man and a woman were sitting on the hood of the car. It hadn't crossed my mind until now that the woman might be the cause of excitement.

"In Turkey, they must look normal," Ali whispered. "They are not accepted here like in America."

The couple went upstairs. The light in the window went off. Ali and I got out of the car. Ali ordered more tea.

It was getting dark. An evening breeze arrived, sweeping out the day's smog. Twenty minutes later, the light upstairs flickered on again.

"I think they're coming down now," Ali said.

I looked up at the window.

"No. Don't look when they come out."

I looked away.

"You can fuck her if you want," Ali offered.

"No thanks," I said. "Ummm, I have a sore throat."

So we finished our tea. There was no more talk of business transactions of any kind. Ali's cousin showed up. I hadn't noticed him slip away, but now he returned with five 20-something French travelers. Ali invited us back inside. His brother and his brother's girlfriend-for-hire had just come down the stairs. His brother's shirt was open, revealing a sweaty chest. I looked at him. He smiled and winked. I looked at the woman. She turned away.

Ali unfurled carpets for the French to admire and sit on. He ordered more tea. Two conversations were going now – one in Turkish between Ali and his cousin, one in French among the new recruits. I sat back and absorbed the moment. Three hours had passed since I'd wandered down this street.

I was relaxing, listening passively, when a word jumped out that scared me. In the garble of Turkish, I caught one word. Ali said it three times in one breath. It was unmistakable. "Hashish...hashish...hashish." He said it with a wide grin.

For the first time in days, my thoughts returned to *Midnight Express*. I had learned over the past two and a half weeks what an unfair picture the movie had painted of Turkey. Nevertheless, I knew not to be around when the pipe came out. My guide book warned of guilt-by-association laws. It said the rumors about drug penalties and Turkish prisons were true. I got up and waited until Ali noticed I was standing.

"It's been great, but I have to go."

He smiled and thanked me for hanging out with him. I thanked him for the tea. I couldn't thank him for the full adventure. He wouldn't understand.

I wandered back to the hostel, at peace with the city and myself again. I hadn't found my shirt, but I didn't care anymore. The day's distractions were far more valuable. A shirt would wear out in time. These memories would stay with me.

The little shop in the hostel courtyard was still open. I went once more to examine the vests I'd seen earlier. I came to the last vest on the rack, the same one I'd spotted before lunch. I hadn't really liked it then. But now it was exactly what I wanted.

I wondered why I had passed it over before. It was beautiful – gray with faded orange stripes, a green and burgundy leafy pattern dyed subtly into one side. The colors were subdued. It wasn't too loud. It fit perfectly. How had I missed it? The thing I'd spent an entire, exhausting day searching for had been right in front of me.

But if I had bought the vest earlier in the day, I would have spent my afternoon waiting to leave the country, drinking beers with other foreigners, complaining about the cab driver and the shoeshine boy who had scammed me. Now I had found exactly what I had been searching for all week. Not clothing. People.

This vest was magical. I was certain of it. It had appeared dull in the morning for a reason. It had sent me on a mission – into the back streets to find the real Istanbul. The vest had sent me out to learn a lesson about my fears and my prejudices. Just as I had started to grow weary in this country, a country that was a challenge to the uninitiated, but a country that had captivated me like no other, this vest had sent me off on one final excursion, one last cultural foray in the city I had once feared. This magic vest had not shown its full beauty earlier in the day because it needed to send me on my day's adventure. Now, it was revealing its true self, and I was certain if I bought it, it would continue working its magic.

PART IV

THE ACCIDENTAL NOMAD

1994-2008

After college, I moved back to Norway to study linguistics. Then I moved back to Madison, where I cobbled together the beginnings of a career as a part-time radio news anchor, part-time exchange student coordinator, part-time translator, part-time freelance writer. I was aching to get overseas again. I started looking for international jobs.

An offer came one day for a two-year contract with an English language newspaper in Saudi Arabia. Was I interested?

"Absolutely," I said.

I was told to be ready to fly to Washington, DC, for an interview. A couple of weeks went by. Then a couple of weeks more. "Keep checking back," they said.

Two months later, I called again. The position was no longer available. The editor had been fired for writing something the king didn't like, and my potential job crumbled along with his.

I applied for teaching jobs – in Ecuador, Greece, and Turkey. The Ecuador job was mine, I was told, as soon as the university obtained funding. Months passed. The funding never came. Finally, I received two different offers from private language schools in Turkey. That was the beginning of my very strange career as a professional nomad.

WHEN SALADS ATTACK

ANKARA, TURKEY

"**I**f there's a free seat next to a man, and a free seat next to a woman, take the seat next to the man. But if the only available seat is next to a woman, it's okay to sit there."

That rule seemed simple enough.

"If you and Natasha get on together and one of the benches has two free spots, you take the middle seat if the person by the window is a man. If it's a woman, Natasha gets the middle."

"Okay," I said, making a mental note.

"Don't pay the driver when you get on. After he starts driving, pass your money to the front."

"Okay."

"And you have to tell the person in front of you how many people you are paying for. *Bir* means one. *İki* is two. *Üç* is three. *Dört* is four."

"Got it," I said, though I really didn't.

"Sit in the back row whenever you can," Phil continued. "If you sit anywhere else, you'll have people passing you money and asking for change. If you're right behind the driver, he'll have a pile of coins for you to make change. It gets complicated when a lot of people have just gotten on."

"Okay."

"And when you're ready to get off, you have to yell."

"All right," I said. "What's the Turkish word for 'stop?'"

"You don't yell 'stop,'" Phil said. "You yell, 'At the corner, there is a person getting off.'"

"Oh. How do you say that?"

"*Yol ağzı inecek var.*"

"*Yola...?*"

"*Yol ağzı inecek var.* Or you can just yell, '*inecek var,*' if that's easier. *İnecek* means 'a person getting off.' *Var* means 'there is.' *Yol ağzı* means 'at the corner.' You can drop that part if it's too complicated. They usually stop at the corner anyway."

The whole thing sounded pretty complicated. "Can't I just yell 'stop?'" I asked.

"No. That's just not the way Turkish works."

The way Turkish worked was making my head spin. Living in Norway had made me a language snob. With Norwegian etched into my brain, and several semesters of college French, I was learning to decipher other European languages without much effort. I had been confident in my ability to master Turkish too, until I arrived in Ankara. The language had no similarities with anything else I spoke. I was slowly memorizing a list of basic survival words – hello, please, bread, cucumber, toilet paper. I could say "thank you" and "where is" and "go away." I was working on "Do you speak English?" and "I don't understand." But the *dolmuş* was too much to keep track of. There weren't just words. There were social rules. There was elementary math, which, in the heat of the moment, became too much for me. People were handing me 50,000 lira notes and saying, "*Üç kişi lütfen.*" To multiply 7,000 lira by *üç* people, and then figure out change for a 50,000 lira note while several other people were also thrusting money under my nose made me feel like the slow kid in math class. I would sigh with relief as I arrived at work. Inside the English school, Turkish was forbidden, even among beginning students.

The word *dolmuş* had two meanings. In this context, it was a minibus. It traveled an assigned route on no particular schedule.

A *dolmuş* would depart once it was filled with passengers, or whenever the driver became too bored to wait any longer.

Dolmuş was also the Turkish word for "stuffed pepper." It was from that food the minibuses took their name – because the buses were stuffed full of passengers.

I wasn't the only English teacher stymied by *dolmuş* lingo. Some teachers refused to ride them alone. They would only ride with other teachers who had lived in Turkey long enough to master the system. This worked as long as you didn't mind being tied to other teachers' schedules, but Phil had told me a story of one guy who relied too heavily on this strategy.

Martin had worked at the school the previous year. He had stayed late after work one day and realized he was going to have to ride the *dolmuş* home alone. He had never learned the phrase to get the driver to stop.

"It's '*Yol ağzı inecek var,*'" Phil had coached him.

All the way home, from the center of Ankara, up the hill into the suburb where most of the teachers had their apartments, Martin practiced the phrase, muttering it quietly enough that no one could hear. "*Yol ağzı inecek var,*" he repeated. "*Yol ağzı inecek var. Yol ağzı inecek var. Yol ağzı inecek var.*"

For 20 minutes, he practiced as the *dolmuş* lurched toward home. Finally, it was time. But somewhere between downtown and home, Martin lost a syllable.

"*Yol ağzı inek var!*" he yelled.

The minibus exploded with laughter.

"Not *yol ağzı* inek *var!*" Phil shouted when Martin came home and asked what he had said wrong. "*Yol ağzı* inecek *var!*"

Instead of shouting, "At the corner, there is a person getting off," Martin had announced, "At the corner, there is a cow."

Turkish had me flustered, but at least my name wasn't posing any problems. "Dave" didn't mean anything in Turkish. My room-mates, Phil and Natasha, weren't so lucky. "Phil" sounded like *fil*, the word for elephant. Natasha came from England, but her name was Turkish slang for a Russian prostitute.

The three of us shared a big, two-story apartment with hard-wood and marble floors, and a balcony that overlooked the city. I began settling into my new life. Every evening after work, I'd hike up a steep hill to the corner market. Nobody there spoke English, which was just what I wanted. They were patient with my infantile Turkish. They would help me add new foods to my vocabulary.

At work, my students liked me – even the level one students, who were learning English from scratch. They were the first class I had ever taught, and slowly, we were learning to communicate.

The teachers were all native English speakers, but we came from all over the world. This confused the students. Classes were in eight-week units, after which a different teacher would step in. Beginning students would just start getting used to my Midwest American accent. Then they'd start unit two with Collin. Collin came from northern Scotland. I could barely understand Collin myself.

One Wednesday morning, after a staff meeting, we all gravi-tated to a Turkish imitation of an American fast food joint. I was doing my best to stick to traditional Turkish grub, but after four weeks away from home, with the other teachers going for burgers, I rationalized I should be social and eat with them.

"That salad bar looks awesome," I said as we entered. It was the first Western-style salad bar I'd seen in the country, stocked with fresh veggies, and dressings hard to find anywhere else.

"I wouldn't do that," Clive warned me.

Clive was a daring eater. A couple of days before, he'd scarfed down a kebab from the shop beneath the school. Every day, scents from all different kinds of kebabs wafted up to the second story teachers' lounge. I'd been told the rule early on: The kebabs tended to cause stomach rebellion. They smelled so good though. Every now and then, somebody would break down and order one, and scarf it down in the teachers' lounge. There would be no scolding the person eating the kebab, and the person eating the kebab would show up for work the next day without complaining about resulting unpleasantries. I had braved one myself, and been fine. But raw vegetables were risky, as was any food that had been sitting out a while.

"You're right," I said to Clive. The Turkish-style salads I was whipping up at home were a safer way to get my vitamins.

I stepped up to the counter. Stretching my language abilities, I ordered a cheeseburger and fries in Turkish. My ego grew as the cashier understood me. She asked in Turkish if I wanted *büyük* (large) or *küçük* (small) fries.

"Küçük," I said.

She asked if I wanted ketchup or mustard.

"Evet, lütfen," Yes, please.

She rattled off another question. I caught one word: *salat.*

In Norwegian, *salat* means plain lettuce as well as a salad. Did I want lettuce on my burger?

Sure. Why not? *"Evet,"* I smiled.

She smiled back and rang up my total. She plopped a burger and fries on my tray. Then she handed me a plastic bowl. I understood what she said from her gestures. "The *salat* bar is over there."

"Oh," I said, falling into English. "I misunderstood. I didn't want the salad bar."

She shrugged and stuck with Turkish. She pointed to the cash register. "You've paid. No refunds."

Clive gave me a scolding look as I sat down with the other teachers. "Dave?"

"I know," I said. "I ordered it by accident."

"You're going to be ill."

"I've been fine with the kebabs."

As I gobbled down the crunchy vegetables, I could tell the other teachers were salivating. Western-style salads like this, with crunchy broccoli, fresh mushrooms and croutons, even Thousand Island dressing, were hard to come by in this part of Ankara. I munched. They scolded. They were jealous.

Phil found me, six hours later, curled on top of my covers in the fetal position.

"Dave," he asked, "are you okay?"

"I'm really sick," I moaned.

"Is it your stomach?"

"Yeah."

I had just spent three hours in the bathroom, undergoing a salad exorcism.

"Do you want to see a doctor?"

"No."

"All right. Maybe a beer would help settle your stomach."

"I don't think so."

"Well give a shout if you need anything. We're in the living room."

I thanked him.

I laid there, shivering and sweating. My whole body ached – like the flu, but with the added feeling that something inside me was very wrong, like a gang of microorganisms was having a bacterial Woodstock. My stomach had been the main stage. Now the rebellious germies were sneaking into other parts of my body to drop acid and reproduce.

My shivering intensified to 6.8 on the Richter Scale. I clutched my arms around my knees in a futile attempt to steady myself. I started to get scared. I needed a doctor.

"Phil!" I heard him in the hallway. My bedroom door was open. I called his name as he walked past.

But the name didn't come out as a shout. It came out as a feeble grunt, a meek gasp that faded into the ether before it ever reached Phil's eardrums. Phil's footsteps faded as he disappeared into the living room.

"Phil," I moaned again, but it was no use. I was so weak, I could barely talk.

Mick Jagger was bellowing from the stereo in the other room. I hated the Rolling Stones. I said a little prayer. "Please, God, if I am going to die, please at least make them put on some better music first."

As "Brown Sugar" came to an end, I realized I was going to have to summon all of my strength. I had about four seconds before the next song would fill the room. Out came another feeble grunt.

"Phil!"

"Dave?" Phil shouted from the living room.

I was too weak to answer.

"Dave?" he shouted again.

"Mmph!"

"Are you okay?"

"No." I tried to shout, but the word wouldn't come out.

"Do you need something?"

I laid there, silent.

Finally, he came to see what was wrong. "You don't look good," he said. "Are you sure you don't want to see a doctor?"

"Yeah. I need a doctor."

Twenty minutes later, a man showed up with a medical bag. He said something in Turkish as he shined a light in my eyes. Phil had lived in Turkey long enough to have a fairly good grasp of the language.

"He thinks you should go to the hospital," Phil translated.

"No," I moaned.

The doctor took my temperature. He showed me the thermometer – 36.4 degrees Celsius. I could convert Celsius to Fahrenheit within a degree or two, but I had no clue what that meant in terms of body temperature.

"That's really low," Phil said.

The doctor leaned over me and looked in my eyes. He spoke his first words of English. "You are going to hospital."

I was too weak to argue.

I was also too weak to move. We lived on the third floor of a building with no elevator. I wasn't sure how I'd make it down the stairs.

Phil and Natasha tried to help me. They each draped one of my arms over their shoulders and coaxed me toward the stairwell, but by the time we got there, my shakes were back.

"I need to sit," I said.

A taxi was honking outside. Phil ran down to ask the driver to wait.

He came back up. "Dave, the taxi's going to leave if we don't hurry."

I couldn't stand though. Even with two people propping me up, it was too painful. So sitting, I slid on my butt, down one cold, marble step at a time. I can't remember how I got from the last step into the taxi, but the next thing I knew, we were speeding through Ankara.

Turks didn't use ambulances much. You had to be closer to death than I was for such luxury. Instead, they would take taxis. It was understood that if a taxi was driving recklessly while flashing its headlights and honking its horn, you should get out of the way.

So that's what was happening. The driver was honking like a road-raging maniac as he sped past the other cars. Too-loud Turkish folk music was screaming from his stereo. Phil was chain-smoking, and spewing his exhaust in my face.

"Are you feeling any better?" he asked.

The next couple of hours were a blur. I remember asking at the hospital if there were any English-speaking doctors, and being told no. I remember a bathroom with neither toilet paper nor soap. Most of all, I remember one word, repeated three times in an otherwise unintelligible sentence. "Cholera...cholera...cholera."

"I have cholera?" I said to Phil in horror. There'd been an outbreak around Ankara, and all I knew about it was it could kill you. In reality, if treated quickly, cholera is highly unpleasant, but rarely fatal. I didn't know this though. All I knew was people died from it, and as I struggled to remain conscious, the word was not comforting.

"They don't know," Phil said. "They want you to go into this other room now."

I didn't know it at the time, but I had just been taken to the worst hospital in Ankara. Good health care was readily available – just not at this joint. On a stretcher, I was wheeled into a big room full of beds. Each bed contained a moaning, writhing Turk. Half of them had digestive emergencies like me. Others had been in car crashes or bar brawls. The doctors parked my stretcher next to a bed and asked me to slide into it. I didn't complain when I saw the blood stains on the sheets. I just wanted to close my eyes.

Phil talked me through the catheter as it went into my arm. "It's sterile," he reassured me. "He's taking it out of a sealed wrapper." The needle was thick, and as it penetrated my skin, for the first time all night, I mustered the energy to really scream.

"You need to hold still," Phil said as the pain subsided. "The doctor can't keep the needle in if you pull away."

"It's not in now?"

"It was but you pulled it out."

The doctor went in for round two. I screamed again, oblivious to the 20-or-so other people in the room who were suffering at least as much as me.

Several hours later, I opened my eyes. I'm not sure if I had lost consciousness or just fallen asleep. The good news was I didn't have cholera. I was just severely dehydrated.

My boss arrived at the hospital around 3:30 in the morning. Mahmut was a pompous man. I didn't particularly like him, but I appreciated him coming to the hospital in the middle of the night.

An hour later, just before the morning prayer calls, he dropped me off at my apartment.

"You can have today off," he said. The next day, however, I was expected back at work.

This posed a problem. Thirty-six hours after the initial outbreak, I had much of my strength back, but not all of it. Walking from the *dolmuş* to school, I had to stop and sit down on the sidewalk. I was still having dizzy spells and my exorcism wasn't quite finished.

Two days after my hospital stay, the lab reports came back illegible. "It either says you tested positive or negative for Giardia," Mahmut's wife, Angela, said. "I can't tell. It says here it was *not* Giardia, but it looks like 'not' is crossed out."

For the next week, I taught my classes, dashing to the toilet at every break. I was losing weight, and I had none to lose. I had only weighed 125 pounds when I arrived in Turkey.

"You look emaciated," Natasha said one day.

The next morning, walking to work, I passed through a park where men hung out with bathroom scales. For a couple of coins, you could weigh yourself. I hopped on. I weighed 45 kilos. I wasn't sure how bad that was until I got to school and did the math. I had lost 25 pounds. I now weighed 100.

I was living on a diet of bread and bananas, dried chick peas, tea and diluted cherry juice. And antibiotics. They'd given me antibiotics at the hospital. I suspected the medicine might be contributing to my upset stomach, but if I did have any of whatever caused the initial problem left in my system, I wanted to zap it. So I popped the pills as directed.

Over the next week, I developed secondary infections. My immune system was sleeping off a post-Woodstock hangover. First came the ear infection. Then the upper respiratory infection. Then, the pains in my groin started. They weren't unfamiliar. I'd had a mysterious, similar pain a couple of years earlier. I had been tested for every possible issue in that part of the body. No cause had ever been found, and after several months, the aches had subsided.

"You must have a UTI," Phil said.

"A what?"

"Urinary tract infection. Try drinking lots of water."

So I did. I started chugging water. The pain worsened. I went to a doctor – a friend of my boss.

"Do you have diabetes?" the doctor asked.

"No."

"I think you have diabetes. Your urine is very clear."

"Yes," I said. "That's because I've been drinking a lot of water."

"Yes!" the doctor smiled, proud of his diagnosis. "If you are very thirsty all the time, it is a sign of diabetes."

"But I'm not very thirsty all the time. I'm just drinking a lot of water."

His smile faded. "Are you married?" he asked.

"No."

"Do you do *coit?*"

"Do I do what?"

"*Coit.*" He gestured – his right index finger through a circle made with his thumb and left index finger – universal sign language for sexual intercourse.

"It's not a sexually transmitted disease," I told him. "I've been very careful."

"In America you have many girlfriends," he informed me. "We must do a test."

In America. Many girlfriends. If only.

I wasn't going to let him test me for STDs. I knew that wasn't the problem. I'd been poked and prodded enough the last few days, and this particular test involved a cotton swab in a place where cotton swabs didn't belong.

"I think we must test you," he said.

"Look," I said, "this is not a sexual disease. I experienced a similar pain a couple of years ago. They tested me for everything then and everything was negative."

So the doctor prodded me in other ways. "I don't think you have cancer," he said.

"Don't *think?*"

He rummaged in his desk drawer. He pulled out some orange pills.

"You need these," he said. "But wait. You should have more. For 10 days." He rattled around in his desk some more. He only had six days worth. He couldn't find any more. He shrugged. "Just take these."

"I'm already taking antibiotics," I said.

"Yes. But those are for your stomach. These are better for your problem."

I went home. I ate dinner and popped a pill. I was starting to feel a little better. In a week, I told myself, everything would be back to normal.

Then, something very abnormal happened.

I went into the bathroom. What came out was not what I would call urine. It looked more like fluorescent orange Kool-Aid, something that had been fermenting inside a nuclear reactor. "This can't be happening," I thought. I didn't know what was causing this psychedelic discoloration. The only thing I could think of was blood. My kidneys were bleeding and I had three hours to live.

"Don't freak out," I told myself as I climbed the hill to the phone booth up the road. I had a phone number for a travelers' medical hotline in America.

"What did you say it's called again?" the nurse asked when I told him about the medicine.

I repeated the name on the box.

"I can't find that in my book," he said.

The package insert was all in Turkish. I scanned for words that sounded like generic drug names.

"Hold on," the nurse said. He put the phone down. For five minutes, I stood in the dark phone booth, wanting to go home to America.

The nurse returned. "Do you have gonorrhea?"

"No."

"Because it says here that medicine is used to treat gonorrhea. And one of the side effects is bright orange urine."

That dumbass! In spite of my protests, the doctor had surreptitiously treated me for many-girlfriends-in-America-itis.

"You mean my urine's *supposed* to be that color if I take this medicine?"

"Says here it's harmless."

The next day at school, I passed the doctor in the stairwell. He had stopped in to visit Mahmut. "How are you feeling?" he asked.

"Ummm, okay. But...." I pulled him into a corner. "Can I ask you something?"

"The color?" he said. I didn't even have to ask.

"Yeah."

"Yes. It is normal."

"Normal?" I wanted to scream. "*Normal?!* You think pissing radioactive Kool-Aid is *normal?!* Why the hell didn't you warn me?!"

I'd come to his office with a mysterious pain in my groin. He had told me I might have diabetes, I *probably* didn't have cancer. He knew how scared I was, yet he neglected to mention this one little "normal" side effect that the tablets were going to give me space mutant urine. And what the fuck was he trying to cure?

"Normal?! I'll show you normal, you...."

I snapped out of my doctor strangulation fantasy. "Thank you," I said.

"Yes. Of course. I'm glad you're feeling better."

I wasn't feeling better. Days passed. My exorcism continued, as did my assorted aches and infections. My mind raced with hypochondriacal diagnoses.

"You need to calm down," Phil kept telling me. "Have a beer."

"I can't drink. The doctor said it will mess up the antibiotics."

"Well do something," Phil said. "Here. Have a fag." He handed me a cigarette.

I didn't smoke, but maybe it was time to start.

I awoke the next morning with bright red splotches all over the back of my throat. I could barely speak.

"Tell Mahmut I'm not coming in today," I said to Phil.

The apartment was empty. I tried to read in bed, but I couldn't focus. I started to cry.

I remembered back to my first Turkish visit five years earlier. I had entered the country paranoid that something bad might befall me if I stayed too long, and instead, I'd discovered a wonderland of friendly people, captivating architecture, and orgasmic cuisine. For five years, I had fantasized about returning. I was back now, living out an adventure I had worked hard to make happen, but instead of the culture shock I had expected, I was dealing with a much bigger emotional challenge – my own hypochondria.

The ear infection, the throat infection, those things I could deal with. But the massive weight loss was scary, and the dull ache in my groin that nobody could diagnose was scarier. "We don't *think* it's cancer" was hardly reassuring from doctors who couldn't fill out a lab report legibly.

Most of all though, I was miserable. Whether my pains were a terminal illness or a psychosomatic nothing, my depression was real. I needed to leave. I needed to regroup and start fresh once I was healthy.

I wanted to do the right thing. I had signed a one-year contract. If I was going to break it, I at least wanted to give fair notice. I had two weeks left in the current unit at school. I'd finish out the unit. Then I'd go home to Madison.

I stayed in bed the rest of the day feeling relieved with my decision. Quitting would be awkward, but it was time. I cringed when I heard Phil's key rattle in the door. He'd understand, but I hated to tell him I was leaving. We'd become good friends.

"How are you feeling?" he asked, poking his head into my bedroom.

"A little better."

"Hey, come in the living room for a moment," he said. That seemed like as good a place as any to break the news.

"Have a seat," Phil said.

I sat.

"Look, Dave, I don't quite know how to say this, but...Mahmut was pissed that you weren't at work today. And, I know this is sudden, but...well...basically you don't have a job anymore."

Mahmut was firing me? For being sick? In this whole ordeal, this was only the second day of work I had missed. I had come all the way to Turkey to work for him, I'd become horribly ill, and he was firing me without even a warning? I was furious. And humiliated. I had never been fired from a job.

"Dave," Phil said, trying to calm me, "you're miserable here. We all feel bad about this, but it's the best thing for you. Go home. Get your health sorted out. Who knows? Maybe you can come back."

Other than Phil and Natasha, I said goodbye to nobody. Ashamed, I fled.

Months later, after way too many medical tests, it was confirmed: I absolutely did not have cancer. My pains were caused by an annoying but harmless condition that was probably triggered by my weakened immune system, and aggravated by stress. The pain persisted for several more months. Then one morning, I woke up and realized it was gone.

For months afterward, I felt depressed. I still loved Turkey in spite of everything. I missed my students. I missed learning Turkish. I missed my daily *dolmuş* rides. But I was terrified to travel now.

This worried me. Foreign travel was my identity. It was something that, until now, I had excelled at. Throughout childhood, I had been a timid kid. Travel was my exception. I dove in fearlessly

– or perhaps fearfully at times, but I still dove in. I had friends who lived vicariously through me, trapped in the white picket fence lifestyles their parents had planned for them. They saw me as the independent one, the intrepid nomad who went and did things they were afraid to. Now, I'd come whimpering home, sickly and depressed. What if this was the end? What if I was too phobic to ever go be foreign again?

But you can't take a squeaky toy away from a poodle. The poodle becomes highly irritable – and far more irritating than the squeaky toy itself. Travel was my squeaky toy, and I was willing to go to desperate measures to get it back.

DRIVING TO EUROPE

INTERSTATE 90, USA

When you interview for a job, it's important to project confidence. Nervousness can be construed as lack of control.

I was a nervous wreck.

I didn't normally get anxious before job interviews, but this was a big one. I was shaking, worried my tongue could seize up at any moment. My interview was about to begin.

"Why do you want this job?" they would ask.

"Derrrrrrr," I would reply, staring blankly as a thin stream of spittle dribbled down my chin. I was competing for the job with several other candidates – people who probably weren't going to drool and lapse into comas during their interviews. I needed to pull myself together. I needed to relax.

I couldn't relax in the clothes I had on. I needed to wear something looser fitting. I'd seem more confident if I felt comfortable. So minutes before the interview, I changed into a less formal outfit: Flannel boxer shorts.

Oh, and I think socks.

"We're a pretty laid-back office," Mary said as we talked on the phone. "If you're a suit-and-tie kind of person, you won't fit in here. We dress casually."

"That's great," I said. "I'm dressed casually right now."

Seventeen months had passed since my Turkish meltdown. My health was back together. I was living in Madison again, working for an educational publishing company. I liked the job, but I was too restless to spend my days in a cubicle. I was interviewing now for a new job with Rick Steves.

Rick's business had grown since my Eurail wanderings five years earlier. He was a TV star now, with thicker guidebooks and a booming tour program. He preached the gospel of budget travel "through the back door." He was fast becoming the benevolent bhagwan of a European travel cult.

For months, I stalked the man, sending him my résumé and writing samples. When a position finally opened, I endured three separate phone interviews with three different supervisors.

My undress for success strategy worked. They hired me without even meeting me in person. All I had to do was drive to Seattle, and the job was mine. I got dressed and rented a U-Haul.

Three weeks later, I was headed toward Minneapolis. So was a massive blizzard.

I had never driven a vehicle this big. I felt nervous with all of my stuff weighing down the back. The sky was growing grayer and angrier by the minute. "Just keep your foot on the gas and try not to hit anything," I told myself. Just in case, though, I had paid extra for collision insurance.

I popped a tape in the stereo as I got on the highway, and I began to relax. It was four hours from Madison to Minneapolis, the one city on my route where I had a friend's couch to crash on. I'd driven this road many times before in the little Honda hatchback I had just sold. I knew the way to Matt's apartment on the shores of Lake Calhoun.

"This isn't bad," I announced to no one in particular as the flurries started to sprinkle the landscape. I rolled through windy farmland. My worries faded. I was going to outrun the storm. Maybe the weather reports had been a bunch of hype. Or maybe the storm had fizzled out.

But the blizzard hadn't fizzled. It was waiting for me, giggling like a nine-year-old kid about to jump out and yell "Boo!" and scare the crap out of me. As I passed the exit for Menominee, Wisconsin, flurries turned to snowballs. There were millions of them, pelting the Wisconsin-Minnesota border as fast as gravity could yank them from the sky. Mother Nature, apparently in a cranky mood, had coordinated her onslaught of snow with the fall of darkness. In minutes, the scene around me transformed from cute, playful flurries that tickled the fields and swirled like squirrels in the road, to darkness, spattered with sinister white blobs of slushy goop. Visibility changed from good to forget-it. Inches in front of me, I could see the snow whapping my windshield. Beyond the windshield, I could make out the blurry red glow of tail lights and the sound of tires crunching in the snow. Traffic slowed to a crawl, until hundreds of motorists were inching forward with nothing to guide them but the tail lights in front of them. That's how we were all navigating – following the car ahead of us, which was following the car ahead of it. Miles ahead, at the front of this impromptu convoy, was a lead vehicle. I wondered where we were following it to. Probably into a ditch.

I thought about pulling off, but the exits were clogged with other frightened motorists. And I knew if I did get off the highway, I might not get back on that night. I drove on.

I awoke the next morning on Matt's couch. Blinding sunshine reflected off the icy lake outside, through the second story living room window, directly into my bloodshot eyes. I rolled over and peered up from my sleeping bag. Matt walked into the room. He didn't say good morning. His first words to me were, "You're not going anywhere today, bro."

"Is it bad?"

"Take a look."

Outside, downstairs, parked in the street, was a U-Haul-shaped blob of snow. The TV channels were doing what TV channels do whenever there's a big storm. They were sending reporters outside to tell the rest of us not to go outside. It was Sunday morning, but already, schools were announcing they'd be closed the next day. I clicked over to the Weather Channel.

"We go live now to Minneapolis, where they picked up 18 to 20 inches overnight. Tom is standing by at Lake Calhoun."

Lake Calhoun? I looked out the window again. There was the camera crew, across the lake, broadcasting live to the nation. You know things are bad when the Weather Channel is broadcasting live from outside your window.

Two days later, roads were still slushy, but I had to go. I started work in six days. I drove until early evening, stopping for the night in Bismarck, North Dakota.

Another, bigger blizzard was stalking me now, aiming for the Dakotas and Montana. I was going to get stranded again. There was no avoiding it. I looked at the map. If I was going to be stuck, it might as well be someplace interesting. There weren't a lot of happening cities between Bismarck and Spokane though. The best I could find was Billings.

Montana's capital had a population of 100,000. I figured they would at least have some nightlife. Two hours beyond Billings was Bozeman, a smaller town, but an okay place. I'd been there years before, on one of those family road trips where you drive around the country and squabble with your elders and siblings. So I had a plan. Shoot for Billings and decide there whether to continue to Bozeman. I wouldn't go beyond Bozeman unless the storm had weakened considerably. Getting stuck anywhere smaller than Bozeman seemed unbearable.

My wake-up call came at five the next morning. Trying to beat the storm, I was driving before sunrise. The air was crisp and chilly. The roads were plowed from the last storm. Like the last storm had started, a few dainty flurries were flittering down.

Late morning, I stopped for gas in a town that had little more than a gas station. A pudgy couple in their early 60s was running the shop. They didn't look like they'd had much business that day.

"Have you heard a weather forecast?" I asked.

"You're good to Billings," the woman said, "but they say it's already coming down hard in the pass. I wouldn't go farther unless you have four-wheel drive."

I took her advice. Ninety minutes later, I pulled into Montana's largest city and drove to the tourist office. A sweet old lady was working behind the counter. I asked if she could recommend a place to stay.

She handed me a list of nearby hotels. "I can call and see if they have a room available," she offered.

"Thanks. I was going to try to get to Bozeman today," I said, making small talk, "but I hear it's bad in the pass."

"Oh no," she said. "I just called the sheriff. The roads are clear."

"Are you sure? Some people told me a little while ago not to go past Billings."

"Well I can call the sheriff again if you want."

How cute. She could just pick up the phone and chat with the sheriff.

"Sure," I said. "If you don't mind."

"It's no trouble at all."

She stood there for two full minutes, phone pressed to her ear, not saying a word. Maybe the sheriff was on his lunch break.

"The recording says the roads are good," she finally said.

Oh. The recording. How old was the recording?

"Are you sure?" I asked.

"You'll be fine."

I got back on the road.

An hour later, I was wanting to turn around. I was wanting to drive back to Billings. I was wanting to go tell the sweet old lady in the tourist office that the sheriff's recording was wrong. Then I was wanting to strangle the sweet old lady for sending me up here. But I was driving up a steep hill, with bald tires, in a truck with everything I owned in the back, on a sheet of ice that hugged the side of a cliff. Turning around seemed risky.

The snow was falling, at least as thick as it had over western Wisconsin three nights earlier. This time, it was daytime, but that didn't help. Asphalt had once again turned to tundra. Bozeman was 80 miles away.

Driving in this sort of weather had been nerve-wracking enough in Wisconsin. In Wisconsin, if you skidded off the road, you'd end up in a corn field. Here, if the weight in my truck suddenly shifted, I was going to go over the edge, tumbling hundreds of feet into a deep crevasse. Oh, sure, there were guard rails. The aluminum kind you sometimes see knocked down along a roadside where a large vehicle, a U-Haul perhaps, has crashed through on its way into the icy ravine below.

Visibility was next to nothing again. Beneath several inches of freshly fallen snow, my tires were skating on glare ice. Suddenly, just feet in front of me, an exit sign appeared. "Big Timber, Montana. Population 1,612."

I had only seconds to think. Pull off or keep going? If I stopped, this would be the end of the line for the night. Conditions would only get worse. Big Timber, Montana? Didn't sound like the most rocking of places, but my instincts told me it was time to stop.

As I drove toward town, it occurred to me a town this size would be scant in accommodations. "I might have to knock on some random door," I thought. The theme music to *Deliverance* started twanging through my head. But ahead, I spotted a motel with a wide open parking lot, practically void of cars. I wondered if it was open.

Here's a helpful winter driving tip: If you are ever in a blizzard in a little mountain village, and you come across a seemingly abandoned motel whose parking lot is buried under six inches of snow, think before you drive your vehicle into that parking lot. Under the six inches of snow, I could not see the four-inch cement barrier that encircled the lot. I heard a loud crunch, which was either my front axle or my spine. My body lurched forward, my front wheels hopped the barrier, and I went into a skid, which lasted about eight feet, until my back wheels slammed into the barrier and stopped. I was straddling the barricade – front wheels on the parking lot side, back wheels on the road side. I was stuck.

There was only one thing to do in a situation like this: Scream. Every obscenity I could think of. Multiple times. I did that for several minutes. Then I remembered the snow was getting deeper.

I tried reversing. The truck would only reverse so far as to get the front tires flush against the barricade. There, they spun, making a noise like a dental drill. *Wrrzhh, wrrzhh, wrrzhhzzz!!*

"Shut the hell up!" I shouted. My truck was laughing at me.

I tried driving forward. I plowed through the snow until my back wheels hit the barrier again. *Wrrzhh, wrrzhh, wrrzhhzzz!!* I had a front-wheel-drive vehicle, with everything I owned weighing down the back. The banjos in my head grew louder.

I had a few different options at this point. One was to yell some more. Another was to spin my wheels futilely and wear down the already meager tread. A third option was to abandon the truck and hike into town for assistance. I decided to go with options one and two.

Wrrzhh, wrrzhh, wrrzhhzzz, went the wheels. I accompanied them with a variety of words, grunts, and whacks to the steering wheel. After several rounds of spinning the tires, getting out of the U-Haul to stare at it, getting back in, and spinning the tires some more, I spotted headlights approaching.

"What kind of idiot would be driving in weather like this?" I wondered.

And then my cynicism turned to love – love for an old cliché. "Neither snow, nor sleet, nor...."

It was the Big Timber mailman, out on his daily route.

I rolled down my window as he slowed to examine my predicament.

"Do you need a push?" he shouted.

"If you don't mind," I yelled back.

If you don't mind? Without this man's help, I was going to die of exposure, alone, in a bare-tired U-Haul, and I was telling him, "If you don't mind."

"When I say so, put it in reverse," he instructed. He waded through the snow and steadied his hands on the hood. "Go!" he shouted.

I stepped on the gas, slowly at first. *Wrrzhh, wrrzhh, wrrzhhzzz!!* I stepped harder. He shoved. I could feel the front of the truck lifting up as it tried to hop the barrier. The tires were lift-ing an inch off the ground, maybe two. Just a little more. Suddenly, wham! I was up, over the barricade, speeding backward across the road toward the trees. I hit the brakes. The truck went into a spin. It slid to an awkward stop. I left the engine running as I jumped out to thank the mailman.

"Hey," I asked him as we said our goodbyes, "are there any *other* hotels in this town?"

"You're lucky you got here," the receptionist said as I checked in to another place a mile down the road. "They just closed the highway."

"Closed the highway where?"

"From Billings to Bozeman."

It was a small, two-story motel with a restaurant across the parking lot – the kind of place where you could order your meat-loaf regular or extra greasy.

"What beers do you have?" I asked after I ordered a burger.

"Miller and Miller Lite," the waitress said. She tapped a Miller into a plastic water glass. "Fries?"

"Sure."

"Where are you headed?" she asked.

"I'm trying to get to Seattle. I'm moving out there, but it's not going too well. I had a little accident with my U-Haul earlier."

A look of horror washed over her face. "Are you the one with the U-Haul?"

"Yeah," I laughed. Had she talked to the mailman?

"The one that overturned?"

"What? No! A U-Haul overturned?"

"About 20 miles down the road. It happened a couple of hours ago. Nobody was hurt but they can't get the truck out. I think they're staying at the motel."

I awoke the next morning to two feet of freshly fallen snow. It was still coming down.

"How are the roads?" I asked at the front desk.

"They've been plowing all night, but the highway's still closed. A U-Haul overturned last night."

"I heard."

I wanted to leave. I couldn't take another day of stranded solitude. There was nothing to do here. The hotel didn't even have the Weather Channel. I was two days behind schedule.

"You're not going anywhere today," the receptionist said. "They don't expect to have the road open till tomorrow morning."

I paid for another night.

"How far are we from the town center?" I asked. I needed something to occupy my day.

"About two miles."

"If I were to hike into town, would there be anything to do there?"

"Not really," the girl behind the desk said.

"Oh."

"There's nothing there but a bunch of bars."

"Perfect."

Downtown Big Timber was about what you'd expect from an isolated village of 1,612 that was trapped in a blizzard. A plow had cleared off the main drag through town. A small grid of side streets and a railroad track were the only other adornments on the map. There was a grocery store, a pizzeria, a bowling alley, and a couple of pubs.

As I trudged through the slush, I spotted a crusty-looking bar. I poked my head in the door. A dozen or so men with stubbly faces looked up from their beverages. Their collective stare said, "You're not from these parts, are you?"

The banjos in my head resumed plunking. I slammed the door and went back into the cold.

I was being ridiculous. I'd wandered into bars in places like Turkey and Latvia and done just fine. I felt more foreign in Big Timber, Montana.

I came upon a lodge with a restaurant and a bar that looked like a place I probably wouldn't get beaten up. I went in for lunch, washed down with a pint of Moose Drool, the local microbrew. This was it. This was the highlight of Big Timber, it seemed. Or maybe there were more exciting parts of town buried in the snow. More sober than I wanted to be, I slogged my way along the service road, back to my motel.

I hiked for an hour. As I got close to home, a truck passed me on the highway. I paid no attention at first. Then it hit me: this was the first non-snow-plow I had seen on this stretch of highway... ever. It was a big 18-wheeler no less. I ran, insomuch as one can run in two feet of snow, back to the hotel reception. A different woman was working now.

"I just saw a truck on the highway," I panted. "Is the road open?"

"They just reopened it."

"Is it safe?"

"For now, yeah. Once it gets dark, it's going to turn to ice."

It was 3 p.m. Bozeman was 60 miles away. I had to get out of here.

"Would it be okay if I checked out?" I asked.

"You've paid for tonight," the receptionist said. "No refunds."

"I paid for tonight because the other receptionist told me the highway would be closed till tomorrow."

"Honey, I can't rent your room this late in the day. Check out's noon."

"Can't rent my room this late in the day?" I wanted to shout. "That's not my problem! It's a freaking blizzard out there!"

But it *was* my problem. They had my money: 35 bucks. If I wanted to escape to Bozeman, I'd have to pay their extortion. My sanity was worth 35 dollars.

By 3:30, I was driving again. The road was wet, but I flew up the hill at a comfortable 50 miles per hour. That lasted about 20 minutes. As I gained in elevation, I started hitting icy patches. I went into a skid on one and realized I needed to slow down. The higher I climbed, the icier it grew, and I abandoned the quiet fantasy that had begun percolating that maybe I'd try to push through to Idaho. I pulled into Bozeman just after sundown. After a night in Big Timber, Bozeman was a metropolis.

The next afternoon, I crossed the border into my new home state. When I reached Spokane, my goal for the day, I kept going, stopping for the night in central Washington. On the final morning of my drive, I hit storm number three.

"Trucks must use chains," flashed a sign above the highway. I just had to cross Stevens Pass, the last stretch of mountains before

Seattle. But I had no chains, and if I did, I wouldn't have known how to put them on anyway. I decided to interpret the sign loosely. If the cops pulled me over, I'd tell them I thought the signs meant bigger trucks. Maybe they really did. Maybe 12-foot U-Hauls with bald tires were allowed.

Over the next couple of hours, as I dropped down to sea level, the snow turned to mist, and then to feeble sunshine. With only minimal utterance of obscenities I made my way through the traffic of a foreign city that was about to become home.

ARRIVAL

PLANET EARTH

Saturday morning: I call my friend Susan to beg for a ride to the airport. I know I can count on Susan because she, like me, is a freelance writer. As my neighbors will confirm, we freelance writers don't really work, and have endless free time to do people favors.

Susan checks her calendar. She is scheduled to do important freelance writer work such as munching bonbons and sipping martinis, but she offers to rearrange her day. She picks me up Monday afternoon and shuttles me through Seattle's rush hour.

At the airport, a lady with a Russian accent checks me in for my flight. She says something about my name and laughs.

"What?" I ask.

"Mr. Fox *Mrrrbllff*," I hear her say.

"I'm sorry. I didn't understand that."

"Mr. Fox Mulder," she repeats. "Do you watch that show, *X-Files?*"

"Oh!" I shout. I double over in laughter.

I can barely breathe, I am laughing so hard. "That's a good one," I gasp. "That's brilliant!" I tell her she should be on Letterman.

I don't really think her joke is funny. I'm schmoozing for an upgrade.

"Hey," I say, wiping tears from my eyes, "I don't suppose you have any 'better seats' available on today's flight?"

"Why yes, we do," she says with a smile. "I can upgrade you to Economy Plus if you like."

It's not business class, but I'm happy. Economy Plus will give me 0.6 extra inches of leg room.

"Wonderful!" I say. "Yes, please upgrade Mr. Fox *Mulder* to Economy Plus! Haha!"

"I'll be happy to," she smiles. "That will be 250 dollars."

Oh.

I should have laughed harder.

I'm doing the math. Do I want to spend 250 dollars just to have a place to put my knees for 10 hours?

"That's okay," I tell her. "Once my legs go numb, I won't really notice the pain."

The good news is this pain will not begin as soon as I expect it to. My flight is delayed two hours. Making productive use of this time, I pace and grumble. Finally, at 8:30 p.m., it's time to board.

Katie is in the window seat next to me. She's a college student traveling to Zürich for a week before she starts a semester abroad in Copenhagen. It's her first trip to Western Europe and she's excited. We compare jetlag strategies.

"Am I supposed to take one Melatonin or two?" she asks after she pops her second tablet.

"I don't know," I say. "I use a different technique."

"What's that?" she asks.

"I follow a special jetlag diet."

She asks what my special jetlag diet consists of.

"As much free alcohol as they'll give you. And a sleeping pill. You can also eat the salmon pasta if you like."

Katie looks skeptical. "I thought alcohol makes jetlag worse," she says.

"It does," I explain. "But the alternative is being awake for 10 hours while the giant behind you keeps kneeing your seat."

Katie orders another glass of water.

Dinner arrives. It's salmon pasta. It's always salmon pasta. I hate salmon. On every eastbound trans-Atlantic SAS flight I've flown on in the last eight years, this is what they have served. It didn't used to be this way. You used to get a choice – usually between artificial beef and artificial chicken. Then the travel industry had a financial crisis and airlines had to cut costs.

So what appears to have transpired is in October of 2001, SAS placed a bulk discount order for a 27-year supply of salmon pasta. I've heard rumors they give you a double portion in business class.

After dinner, I doze. When I wake up, it's 3 a.m. Only it's not really 3 a.m. It's already lunch time in Europe. I look at the in-flight map on the video screen. We're zooming over Reykjavík.

The video map is a relatively new invention. It shows where in the world you are, and offers statistics such as your speed, how much time is remaining in your flight, and how many feet you will plummet to your death if the engines fail.

Breakfast is served. It includes the most delicious ham I have ever tasted. But that's all psychological. Anything tastes good after the salmon pasta.

In Copenhagen, we're greeted with chaos. Hundreds of passengers have missed connecting flights due to the delay in Seattle. There's a long line at the customer service desk.

I spot Katie and pull her out of the line. "Follow me," I say. "I know another place in the airport where the line won't be so bad."

We get there, and there is no line at all. This is because this other desk is closed. A sign instructs us to hike 17 kilo-meters through the airport to a third desk.

CPH is a sprawling airport with a shopping mall, a mini hotel, a sauna, and a multi-denominational prayer room where you can ask the deity of your choice to please create some better airline food. The airport is so big, employees cruise from one end to the other on scooters.

COWCHINPIG: god of non-fish-eating travelers and muckrakers everywhere

Katie and I make the trek on foot. A man books me on a new flight to Stockholm, departing at 5 p.m. I wish Katie well and set off alone to find my next flight.

At quarter to six, the pilot announces we will land soon. I'm happy to hear this because I have resorted to drinking water – lots of it – and my bladder is beginning to ache. Fifteen more minutes. I can hang on that long.

But something is wrong. We are not descending. We are circling – doing laps, around and around the same cloud. Earlier thunderstorms in Stockholm have caused a traffic jam in the sky. We are seventh in line to land.

"Please remain seated with your seatbelts fastened," the pilot announces over the loudspeaker. "And no, Mr. Fox Mulder, you may not go to the lavatory."

Forty-five minutes and a bladder infection later, I am on the ground in Sweden. I just need to collect my bags.

I find the conveyor belt and wait.

And wait.

And wait.

Nothing is happening. Twenty minutes pass. No bags arrive. Thirty minutes pass. Forty minutes. A lady comes and asks me what is taking so long.

I'm not sure why she's asking me. My suspicion, however, is that she has noticed how exhausted I look, and thinks it will be fun to ask me irritating questions... in Italian.

"I don't know," is all the Italian I can muster. "There is a problem."

She proceeds to tell me her entire life story. Every few minutes, I smile and tell her, "I don't understand," so she knows I am paying attention.

After an hour and 10 minutes, the bags arrive. At 8:30 I am at the Hotel Wellington, my home in Stockholm.

Gunhilla, my favorite receptionist, is waiting for me at the desk. "You made it!" she smiles.

Lightning has zapped part of the hotel's wiring. "There's only one room on the top floor that has electricity," Gunhilla tells me. "But we saved it for you because we know you like it up there."

Dizzy from exhaustion, I take a hot shower. I'm too tired to go out for dinner. Instead, I go to the hotel bar for pizza.

"Is everything functioning okay in your room?" Gunhilla asks as she hands me a menu.

"Yes," I tell her. "Everything but me."

As I look over the menu though, I realize I have finally arrived in a happy place. There are dozens of pizza toppings to choose from. And none of them is salmon.

I never intended to end up here. It's been a long journey.

When my parents stuck me on my first international flight in 1976, I had no idea how drastically life was about to change. Travel will do that to you. You think a trip's got a finite timeframe, but one journey leads to another, and the next thing you know, the once-magical experience of flying overseas has turned into a whinefest about economy class legroom.

"I'll tell you what," my brother said to me the other day. "If it would make you feel better, let's trade jobs. My cubicle at work has awesome legroom."

My job requires that I cross oceans several times a year now. These days, I eat the airline food, but I still grumble about it. I roll my eyes at the flight safety video, which is like a bad television rerun I've seen 129 times. I dread the impending jet lag and swollen feet. I wallow for a few moments in "here we go again" self-pity

– 10 droning hours from Seattle to Europe. I can only wallow for so long, however. As the plane pulls away from the gate, a giddy energy wafts through the recycled air.

Each passenger is here for a reason. Some are on business trips. Some are going to visit family. Some are on their first, life-altering forays into foreignness, and their excitement is palpable. It permeates my curmudgeonly mood.

I don't travel like a normal tourist anymore. Museums and monuments no longer excite me. Neither do towering cathedrals. But tell me the story behind the people who built the buildings, painted the paintings, suffered while alive to be honored with statues centuries after their death, and I get goose bumps. It's the people on our planet that enthrall me. It's the people so different from me who teach me stuff. In lucky moments when I'm far from familiarity, I stumble across magical exchanges on an intimate, one-to-one scale.

A black-clad widow on a train in northern Greece doesn't know my language, so instead of saying hello, she offers me a quince, and a paring knife to slice it with. We trade smiles as I crunch into the bitter fruit. She probably does not realize the free snack she plucked from a roadside tree will keep her alive in my memory* years after she has left this world.

and in an extremely weird travel book

A 20-something border guard in the former East Germany stops me at customs, and I can't help but notice how cute she looks in her military uniform. When she was a young child, our governments were telling us not to trust each other. I think she wants to see my passport, but that's not what she's after. She wants a sniff of the amaretto-doused crepe I just purchased down the road. I offer her a bite. She laughs and waves me across the border.

A crazed farmer in Dingle, Ireland, orders me to help him catch his runaway sheep. But I'm from the suburbs. Sheep wrangling is not part of my repertoire. So I fake it. I pretend I want to help tackle the woolly beast, though secretly, I am rooting for the sheep. Eventually the farmer figures out whose side I'm on. He grabs the sheep by the horns and says to the animal, "Come on, Lucy. Let's go home." I give Lucy a wink as we part company.

An aging beggar in Hammamet, Tunisia, sits with an outstretched palm, outside the entrance to the walled city. I look in his eyes, then down at his feet. A spark crackles in my memory. I've met this man before. He is in the same spot where he sat in 1976, with the same, unforgettable feet-turned-inward. I hand him a one-dinar coin, and he thanks me in French. I'm too shy to tell him I remember him from my childhood visit, countless journeys ago.

At a hole-in-the-wall restaurant in Athens, Greece, the cook invites me back into his kitchen. He speaks not a word of English, but he knows all the English versions of animal noises. *"Baah, baah,"* he says, pointing to a steaming pot of stewed lamb. He points to another pot and clucks like a chicken. I smile. It's a beautiful thing when two people from disparate cultures transcend language barriers by clucking like chickens.

These moments happen most often when I abandon the tourist-trodden main arteries and get a little lost. Getting lost has become my favorite thing to do when I travel. My best adventures are the accidents, the things I stumble upon because my plans have run amok. I don't care where I end up, as long as there's a stranger to meet. Every person on our planet has stories to tell, and our own lives become much more interesting when we tangle up our stories with the stories of strangers.

This is part of the reason I became a tour guide. I want lots of people from lots of places to all get to know each other. If more people on our planet would get together in simple ways, transcending politics with bites of fruit, nibbles of crepes, shots of tea, or swigs of the local *aqua vitae*, if more of the world's people would come together and cluck like chickens, we might not bomb each other so much.

Oh, but let's not get carried away. This is no time to start singing "We Are the World." This is my book, and I will not allow such behavior. Besides, tour guiding is more than just a bunch of touchy-feely, world-peace-inspiring moments. I told you my travel philosophy at the beginning of this book: "When you travel, things go wrong."

When you travel with 28 people following you, things go wrong times 28. As a tour guide, it's my job to fix them – or better yet, to keep my groups oblivious to what's unraveling behind the scenes. I contend with all sorts of challenges – lost luggage, lost passports, medical emergencies, dental emergencies, bus breakdowns, mental breakdowns, bus crashes, transportation strikes, missing hotel reservations, overbooked night trains, renegade rodents, legal threats, physical threats, bathroom emergencies, missing people, people who don't shower and terrorize the rest of the group with their stench, people who are terrorized by said stench and want *me* to tell the offender he or she reeks, surly restaurant owners, flooded hotel rooms, ugly Americans, ugly Europeans, worriers, stragglers, chronic complainers, and questions. Lots of questions.

What floor will the rooftop picnic be on? Can I take a train from France to the south of France? Can I take a day trip from Munich to Australia? Which restaurants in London will be serving a vegetarian Thanksgiving dinner? What town is the Leaning Tower of Pisa in? Are the views from the train better in first class? Can I catch Mad Cow Disease if I eat French ham?* People have asked me all of these things.

The answer to that last question is, "Oink."

Then there are the not-so-goofy questions – legitimate questions I just can't answer. Trees are my weakness. For reasons I do not understand, people really want to know about trees. "What's that tree called?" they ask, and the only answer I can come up with is, "Herman. That tree is called Herman."

I can tell you all about the Vikings, the Etruscans, and why we drive on the other side of the road from the British.** I can talk about the animals that roamed Europe thousands of years ago, the history of the European Union, the

It's Napoleon's fault.

bright side to the Bubonic Plague, the moral system of the Gypsies, and more about Abba than you'd ever want to know. But when it comes to trees, I barely know the difference between an oak tree and a cactus.

But "What kind of tree is that?" is a common question. Once somebody got really specific. She asked me, "What kind of *oak* tree is that?"

"It's a Danish Oak," I answered. It seemed as good an answer as any. We were in Denmark.

"Oh," she said. "Is that a kind of oak tree?"

YUM!   "It sure is."

People often say to me, "You should write a book about the people on your tours. That would be a really funny book, Dave." What they really mean by this is, "You should write a book about all the evil jerks on your tours."

But that's not how most of the people are on my tours. Most of the people on my tours are kind and rational.* I've guided some fascinating people around Europe – Broadway musical directors, Olympic medal winners, even Michael Jackson's orthodontist.

True, over the years, I've worked with a few thousand people in foreign countries. Statistically, it's inevitable there would be a few challenging personalities. Goofy questions? I can live with those. Hey, if we have the courage to step out of our cultural comfort zones at all, we're all entitled to ask a goofy question or two. It's the aggressive questioners who rattle me, the ones who start sentences with, "Why didn't you tell us…."

*Besides, if I wrote a book about the handful of evil jerks who have infiltrated my groups over the years, the evil jerks would sue me. That's what evil jerks do.

"Why didn't you tell us there's an exhibit of 14th-century kidney stones at the Museum of Obscure and Gross Medical Stuff?" the aggressive questioner might ask.

"Ummm, I didn't know such a museum existed."

"Well it does. I found it on the Internet. It's only 25 minutes from the city center and it's the best museum east of Vladivostok. Why hasn't Rick Steves put it in his guidebook?"

These situations invariably show up in my tour evaluations. "Dave was the worst tour guide ever. When I asked him about the history of 14th-century kidney stones, he promised me he'd look it up and get back to me, and he *never did!!!!!!!!!!*"

Then there are people like Pearl. Pearl (not her real name) was on the first tour I ever worked on as an assistant guide. She made it clear one evening that if she tripped during the night, on her way to the bathroom in the dimly lit hotel hallway, she would sue the hotel and Rick Steves. To appease her, I offered her my flashlight.

"Well, shit!" she yelled as I was walking away. "How do you turn this damn thing on?"

I went back to help her, but the batteries had died. My flashlight had turned itself on in my backpack.

"I'm sorry," I said. "I don't have any more batteries."

Pearl smiled a victorious smile. Then she hissed, "Now I see why you're the *assistant* guide."

So yes, over the years, I've encountered a few toxic tour members, but most of the people I work with are remarkably patient. Most of them get it that I'm human – and therefore entitled to my own bouts of stupidity.

One time in Sweden, I announced the wrong departure time for our overnight train to Stockholm. It was an honest mistake – there had been a last-minute schedule change – but an "honest mistake" did not soften the fact that my entire group was about to be stranded, with no place to sleep for the night. I sprinted through the city of Malmö, frantically spreading word that we needed to meet at the train station earlier than I had announced. As I panted down the pedestrian-packed main street, scanning outdoor cafés for familiar faces, I tried to compose a back-up plan: What would I do for the people I couldn't locate in time? Would I stay behind and help them, or travel with those who did show up and keep the tour on schedule? But no such plan was revealing itself. My mind was numb with panic. At 12 minutes to departure, I gasped my way into the station, still not sure what I was going to do. The entire group greeted me at our predetermined meeting point with applause and a bottle of wine. They had all found each other. We caught our train.

On another occasion, I had given my group a stern warning we needed to be punctual in the morning. We needed to be on the road by 7:30 or our day would not go off as planned. At 7:37, my hotel room phone yanked me from a deep slumber. It was the bus driver.

"Dave, where are you?" *In my room! Duh!

I packed in record time and boarded the tour bus nine minutes later. Had I been clear-headed, I would have concocted a story about an emergency phone call from home that delayed me, but I was too groggy to weave such a tale. All I could offer was a profuse apology.

Rolling out of Oslo, someone in the group handed me a sandwich and a double shot of espresso. "Relax," she said. "You're human."

She was right. I am human. So are you. So are most of the other people on this planet.* And most of us are good people. It's just that sometimes, we don't get each other. That's why we need to travel. We need to meet each other. We need to go out in the world, get a little lost, cluck like chickens and see what we find. It's often the things we didn't realize we were looking for, because we didn't even know they existed when we first set out on a journey, that end up creating our best stories. Journeys end, but our stories stay with us.

* The jury is still out on Michael Jackson.

You've just endured a few of my stories. I have many more, and if you can convince your 5,693 closest friends to each buy 328 copies of this book, maybe I can publish a sequel someday. Until then, it's time for me to go.

Where am I going now? To one of my favorite places in the whole world: My refrigerator. I'm going to make myself a sandwich, pop open a beer, and then migrate to my couch where I will spend my Friday night watching some bad reality television.

That's what I do when I'm not working in foreign places. I stay home and savor the weeks when I get to sleep in my own bed. I revel in the boredom. When I'm home for too long, I do get antsy. I do look forward to my next knee-cramping plane ride. But I've traveled enough now that the sweetest part of any journey is the moment when I land back in Seattle and ride home from the airport. As I arrive at my front door, I stand there for a minute and delight in the thought that behind that door is my very own bed. Finally, after weeks away, I am going to get to snuggle under my old, familiar, flannel comforter...if only I could remember where the hell I packed my keys when I left for the airport two months earlier.

You should go make a sandwich too. You look hungry. Then maybe you should plan a trip, go tangle up some stories of your own. I know – if you don't work in the travel industry, getting yourself overseas isn't quite so easy. But if you don't start dreaming, stashing away a little money, checking out guidebooks from the library, and perfecting your chicken imitations, the next thing you know, your favorite bad TV show is going to be in reruns, stale like a flight safety video, and you'll wish you had something else to do.

So go! Go get lost, and see what you find. There is chaos out there to be savored. Sure, leaving the snug safety of your familiar world can be scary sometimes, but don't worry. I've checked, and you can still bring your blankie through airport security.

ABOUT THE AUTHOR

D
ave Fox is an award-winning humor and travel writer and public speaker. Originally from the United States, he has lived in England, Norway, and Turkey (but not all at the same time), and traveled in roughly 40 countries. He has devoted his life to exploring foreign cultures and trying not to make a mess of things.

In 2004, Dave won the Erma Bombeck Writers' Workshop Book Proposal Contest. *Getting Lost: Mishaps of an Accidental Nomad* is his resulting collection of humorous stories about things that have gone wrong in his international wanderings.

Dave is a veteran tour guide for European travel guru Rick Steves, and a former public radio news anchor. He has been an opening speaker for Princess Märtha Louise of Norway, and he has been featured on the History Channel television program, "Weird US," as an anti-lutefisk activist.

His work has been published in books by Rick Steves and Lonely Planet, in a variety of national magazines and newspapers, and in letters to his mother, though not often enough if you ask her. He has also produced an audiobook CD, *The Fox that Quacked: Essays from Planet Earth*, which is available on his humor website at DAVETHEFOX.COM.

His latest book, *Globejotting: How to Write Extraordinary Travel Journals (and still have time to enjoy your trip),* will be published by Inkwater Press in the summer of 2008.